KINGFISHER KNOWLEDGE

SPEED MACHINES

AND OTHER RECORD-BREAKING VEHICLES

KINGFISHER KNOWLEDGE

SPEED MACHINES

AND OTHER RECORD-BREAKING VEHICLES

Miranda Smith

KINGFISHER
NEW YORK

KINGFISHER
Published in the United States by Kingfisher, an imprint of Henry Holt and Company LLC, 175 Fifth Avenue, New York, New York 10010.
First published in Great Britain by Kingfisher Publications plc, an imprint of Macmillan Children's Books, London.

Distributed in Canada by H. B. Fenn and Company Ltd.

Library of Congress Cataloging-in-Publication Data has been applied for.

ISBN: 978-0-7534-6287-4

Kingfisher books are available for special promotions and premiums. For details contact: Director of Special Markets, Holtzbrinck Publishers.

First American Edition May 2009
Printed in Singapore
10 9 8 7 6 5 4 3 2 1
1TR/1108/TWP/MA(MA)/130ENSOMA

Contents

Chapter 2

Water transportation 31

Chapter 3

Air transportation 45

NOTE TO READERS

The Web site addresses listed in this book are correct at the time of going to print. However, due to the ever-changing nature of the Internet, Web site addresses and content can change. Web sites can contain links that are unsuitable for children. The publisher cannot be held responsible for changes in Web site addresses or content or for information obtained through third-party Web sites. We strongly advise that Internet searches are supervised by an adult.

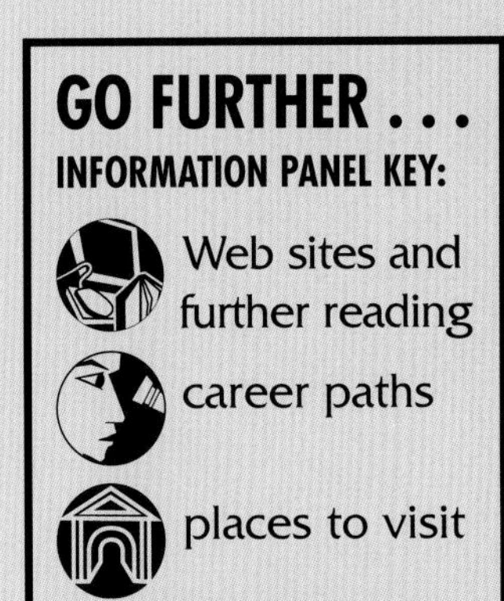

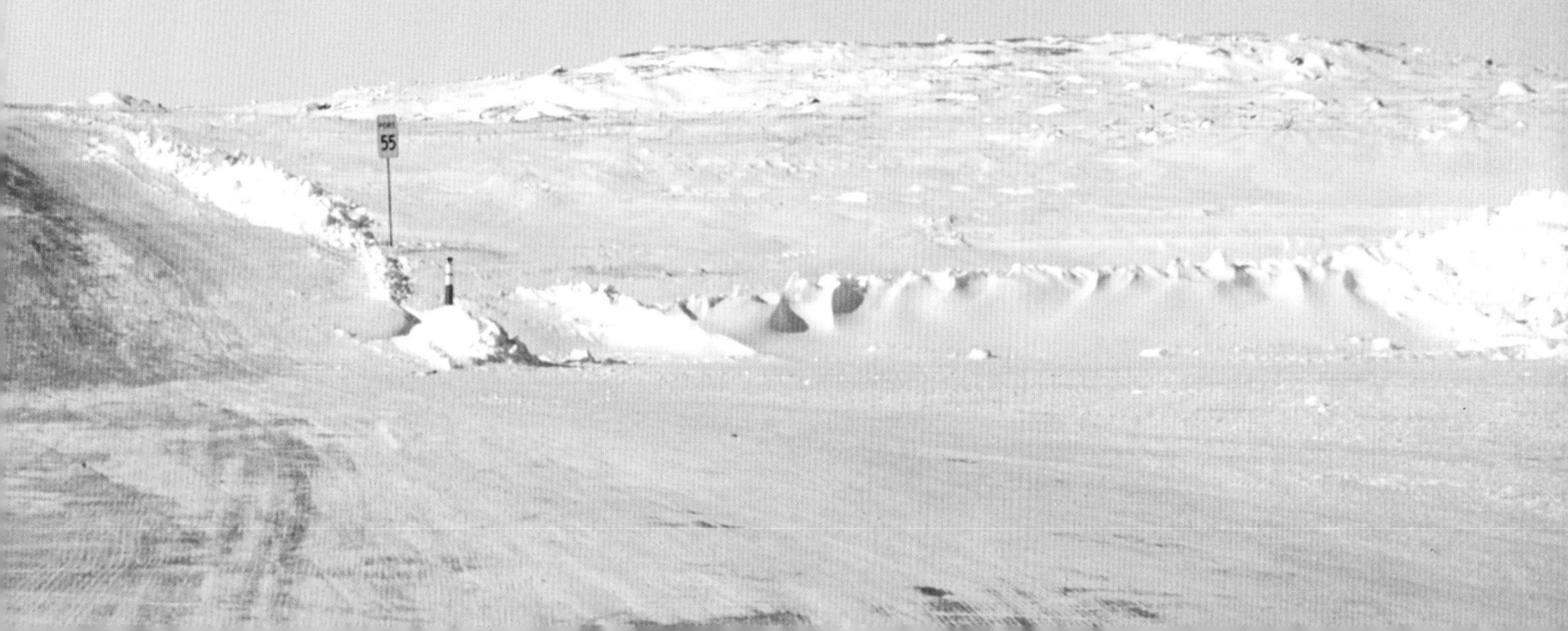

▼ In northern Canada, a truck approaches the frozen surface of a lake along the route of the longest ice road in the world.

Foreword

On February 7, 2005, I became the fastest person to sail around the world alone. Incredibly, I had broken what many (including me) thought was an unbreakable record, racing around the planet in my 75-foot (23-m) trimaran *B&Q* in 71 days, 14 hours, 18 minutes, and 33 seconds.

It all began at the age of four, when I was introduced to sailing by my aunt Thea. Stepping onboard her boat *Cabaret* for the first time triggered something inside me that has never left. It was the start of a passion for sailing and the water that has lasted my whole life!

As a kid I dreamed of sailing solo around the world, and I spent a huge amount of time reading about famous sailors such as Sir Francis Chichester (1901–1972) and Sir Robin Knox-Johnston (born 1939). I was so inspired by them that I even saved up my lunch money to buy my first boat! I loved the freedom that sailing gave me out on the water, with the prospect of being able to sail wherever I wanted in the world.

I am absolutely fascinated by learning, and I always want to push myself to learn more about sailing and to really understand the boats on which I am sailing. I am also quite competitive and want to race my boats as fast as possible, so trying to break records was a natural progression for me.

Records are set to be broken, however, and in January 2008, Frenchman Francis Joyon took back his solo nonstop around-the-world record. I really had to give everything to beat his 2004 record, but now he has bettered mine by 14 days through a combination of a bigger, faster boat, ideal weather, and outstanding seamanship.

Francis's journey was also a way for him to send a message regarding the planet and its preservation. He relied only on clean energies such as wind and solar power and did not have an engine aboard his trimaran, which fantastically illustrates what can be achieved. High-speed travel has enabled us to see that the world is not really all that big after all and that we have an urgent need to protect it—apart from anything else, so that future generations can set their own speed records!

I hope that all the amazing stories about record breaking in this book will inspire you, too, so that one day you can break your own record. If, like Francis Joyon, you can do it using clean energies, then that would be truly awesome!

Go for it!

Ellen MacArthur, British yachtswoman who in 2005 broke the record for the fastest solo nonstop voyage around the world on her first attempt.

Chapter 1

Land transportation

The air is full of dust, the ground vibrates, and there is a deafening scream as engines speed past along the racetrack. There is nothing as exciting as super-fast Formula One cars battling to win a race on a hot summer's day.

Throughout history people have competed to reach the finish line first. The invention of new types of transportation and the development of new technologies in the 1800s and 1900s meant that people and machines could work together in order to achieve feats and speeds that had previously been impossible. Every year, history is made and new records are broken. Only the best reach their goal, whether that be as a cyclist in the grueling Tour de France, a trucker in the dusty Dakar Rally, or a motorcyclist battling for a podium place in the MotoGP World Championship.

British Formula One star Lewis Hamilton leads the race in his McLaren MP4/23 at the 2008 German Grand Prix.

High-speed travel

On October 15, 1997, British Royal Air Force fighter pilot Andy Green drove *Thrust SSC* (SuperSonic Car) into the record books at an extraordinary 761.35 mph (1,227.99km/h). He made two "runs" in the Black Rock Desert, Nevada, breaking the sonic barrier both times. This amazing vehicle has two Phantom jet engines that take around 30 seconds to get *Thrust* up to supersonic speed. *Thrust SSC* was designed by the previous record-holder, Richard Noble, who had reached 632.07 mph (1,019.47km/h) in *Thrust 2*.

▲ Former test astronaut Gary Gabelich drives *Blue Flame* up to 621.04 mph (1,001.67km/h) on the Bonneville Salt Flats, Utah. The rocket-powered, bullet-shaped car broke the land speed record on October 23, 1970. *Blue Flame* was 37 ft. (11.3m) long. It was fueled using a highly explosive mixture of liquid natural gas and hydrogen peroxide, so it did ride on a blue jet of flame.

Obsessed with speed

People are always pushing boundaries, and the men who have broken the world land speed record have pushed them further than most. During the 1960s, the world land speed record passed back and forth, as two Americans fought it out on the Bonneville Salt Flats. Art Arfons earned the title three times in *Green Monster*, while Craig Breedlove triumphed four times in *Spirit of America*. Their dominance was broken in 1970, when Gary Gabelich zoomed to victory in *Blue Flame*.

▶ *Thrust SSC* was the result of two and a half years of research, followed by around 100,000 hours of construction. It is the first car to use two turbojets, and it weighs 11 tons (10 metric tons). It can accelerate from 0-99 mph (0-160km/h) in four seconds. By using very strong ribbon parachutes, *Thrust SSC* is slowed down to a speed at which the brakes can be used safely.

aerodynamic shape like a twin-jet fighter aircraft with the wings removed

Staying grounded

The engineers working on *Thrust SSC* had to figure out how to prevent the car from taking off into the air. Air rushing over its streamlined surfaces created lift, forcing it upward. When compensating for this, they had to be careful not to let the nose grind into the ground. They also knew that the shock waves caused by breaking the sonic barrier would hit the ground under the car, and they had to prepare for the possible dangers to the car and its driver that this could cause.

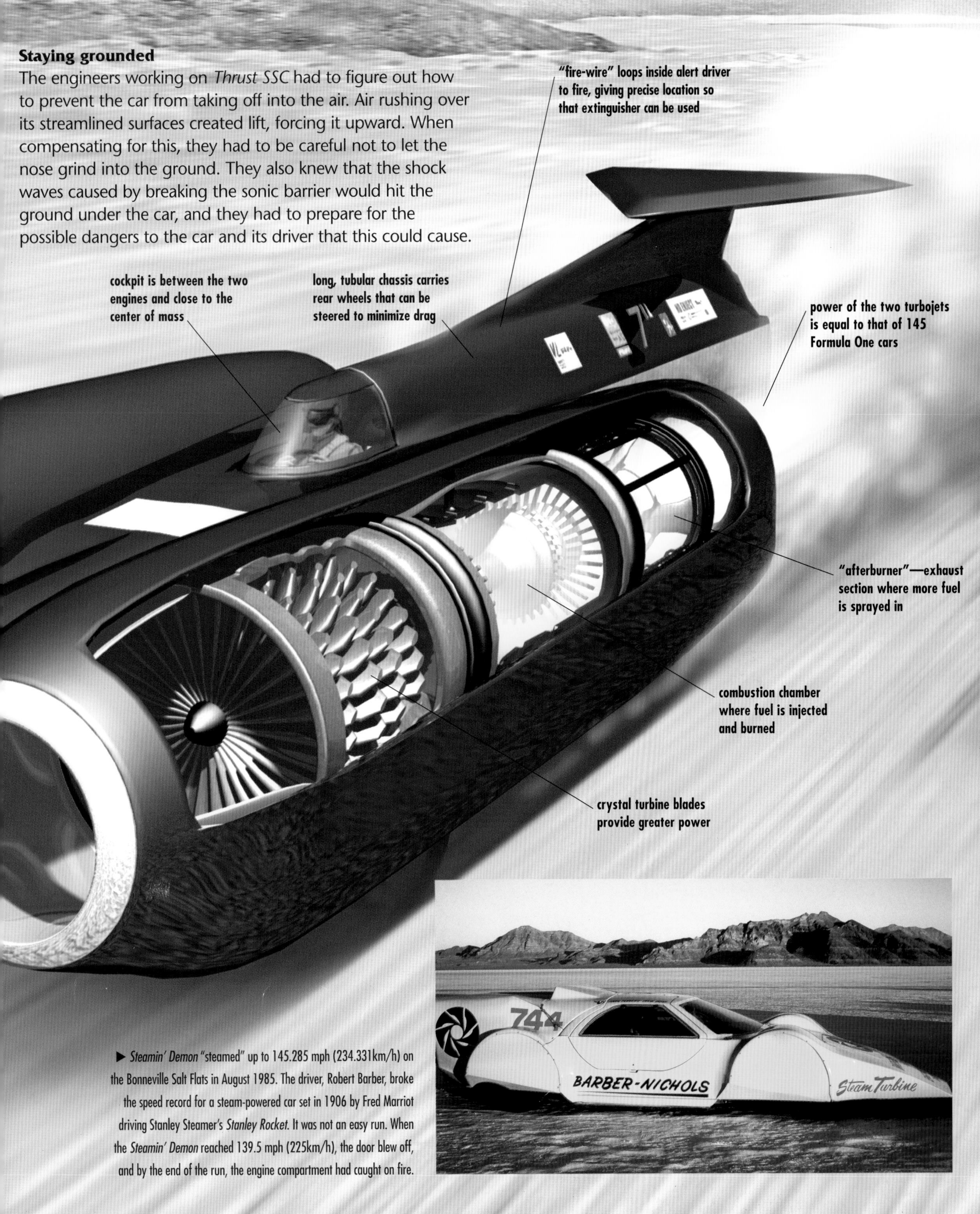

"fire-wire" loops inside alert driver to fire, giving precise location so that extinguisher can be used
cockpit is between the two engines and close to the center of mass
long, tubular chassis carries rear wheels that can be steered to minimize drag
power of the two turbojets is equal to that of 145 Formula One cars
"afterburner"—exhaust section where more fuel is sprayed in
combustion chamber where fuel is injected and burned
crystal turbine blades provide greater power
744
BARBER-NICHOLS
Steam Turbine

► *Steamin' Demon* "steamed" up to 145.285 mph (234.331km/h) on the Bonneville Salt Flats in August 1985. The driver, Robert Barber, broke the speed record for a steam-powered car set in 1906 by Fred Marriot driving Stanley Steamer's *Stanley Rocket*. It was not an easy run. When the *Steamin' Demon* reached 139.5 mph (225km/h), the door blew off, and by the end of the run, the engine compartment had caught on fire.

The "fastest man on Earth"

On December 10, 1954, Captain John Stapp of the U.S. Air Force became the fastest man in the world—a record that has yet to be broken. Scientist Stapp used himself as a guinea pig to test the effects of acceleration and deceleration (g-force) on the human body. In *Sonic Wind No. 1*, a rocket-propelled sled built out of welded tubes, he reached a speed of 6,402 mph (10,326km/h).

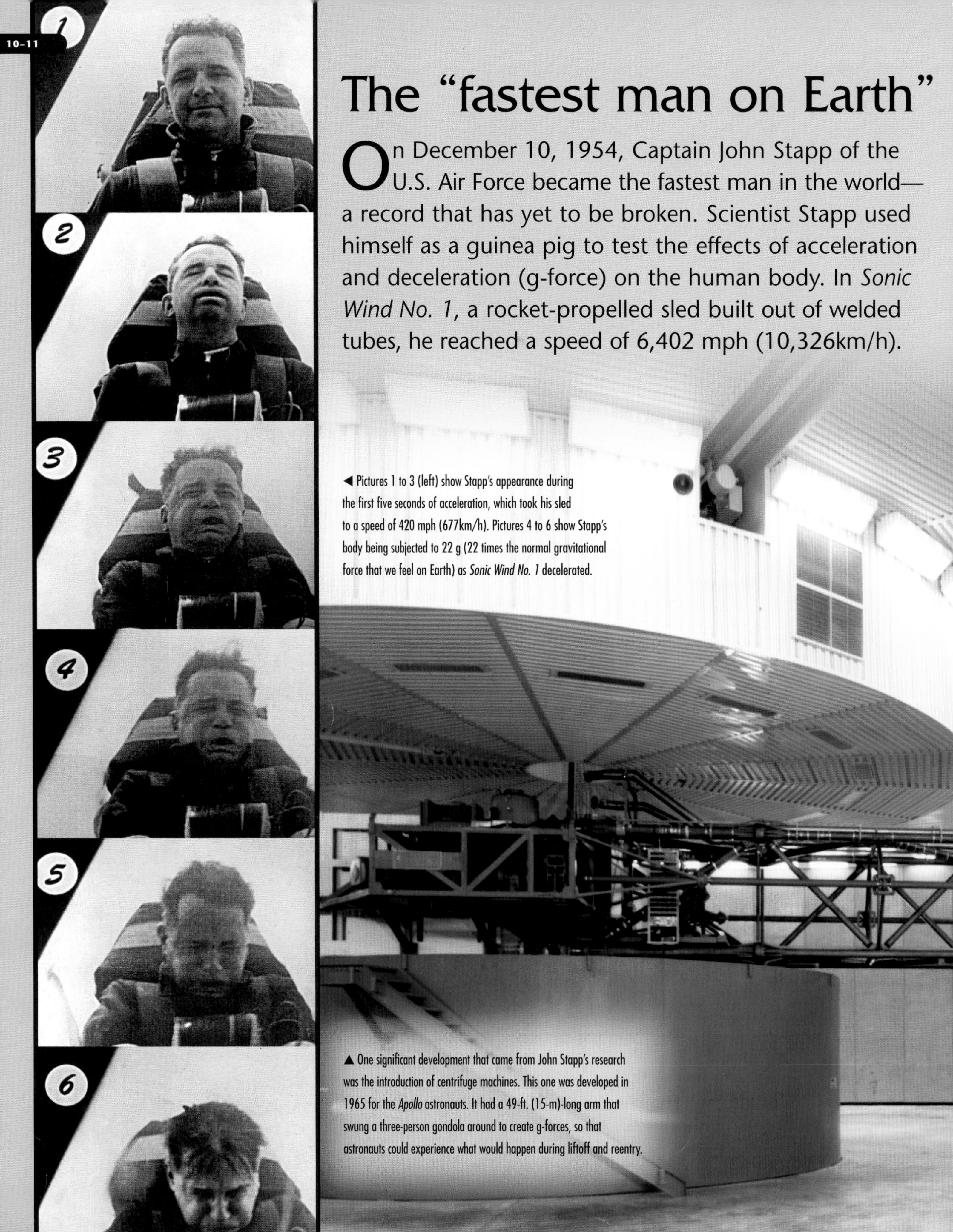

◀ Pictures 1 to 3 (left) show Stapp's appearance during the first five seconds of acceleration, which took his sled to a speed of 420 mph (677km/h). Pictures 4 to 6 show Stapp's body being subjected to 22 g (22 times the normal gravitational force that we feel on Earth) as *Sonic Wind No. 1* decelerated.

▲ One significant development that came from John Stapp's research was the introduction of centrifuge machines. This one was developed in 1965 for the *Apollo* astronauts. It had a 49-ft. (15-m)-long arm that swung a three-person gondola around to create g-forces, so that astronauts could experience what would happen during liftoff and reentry.

Aviation breakthrough

John Stapp was a qualified doctor who was determined to find ways to protect pilots at very high altitudes. He had already discovered how to stop pilots from getting "the bends"—deadly bubbles that form in the bloodstream at great heights and depths. By experimenting on himself, he found that if the pilots breathed pure oxygen for 30 minutes before takeoff, they would not suffer from the bends at all.

▶ The record for the fastest speed traveled on the Moon was set on April 23, 1972. U.S. astronaut John Young drove *Apollo 16*'s Lunar Rover 10.53 mph (16.99km/h) in what came to be known as the "Grand Prix run."

Dangerous testing

In 1946, Stapp was the flight surgeon to U.S. test pilot Chuck Yeager when Yeager broke the sonic barrier in a Bell X-1 aircraft at Mach 1. Afterward, Stapp planned his rocket-sled experiments to develop a harness that would hold pilots safely while in g-force conditions. The first sled was named *Gee Whiz*. During the tests, Stapp lost fillings in his teeth, fractured his ribs, broke his wrist twice, and damaged his eyes.

▼ *Sonic Wind No. 1*, Stapp's second rocket-powered sled, is seen here in action during its record-making run in Holloman Air Force Base, New Mexico, in 1954. It ran along a 2,000.8-ft. (610-m)-long track. At one end were sets of hydraulic brakes that slowed the sled from 150–75 mph (240–120km/h) in one fifth of a second.

sensors on harness measured g-force when rocket came to sudden stop

A winning formula

Motor racing is one of the most exciting sports, and the annual Formula One World Championship inspires millions of fans all over the world. The cars are the most technologically advanced—and the most expensive. The race is for open-wheelers—cars that are specially built and have their wheels outside the body of the car. The drivers compete to become the World Drivers' champion, while their expert team of engineers aims to win the World Constructors' trophy.

▲ In contrast to Formula One cars, early stock cars were ordinary cars off the factory production line with finely tuned engines. Today, the cars competing in the very popular NASCAR races in the U.S. (above) have eight-cylinder engines and travel around an oval track at more than 186 mph (300km/h).

Racing start

Formula One racing usually takes place on purpose-built racetracks, and two cars from each team participate. There is a qualifying round to decide the lineup on the grid, and who will hold pole position—the best place from which to start the race. The cars are made from carbon fiber, which is lightweight but strong. They can accelerate from 0–60 mph (0–100km/h) in less than three seconds.

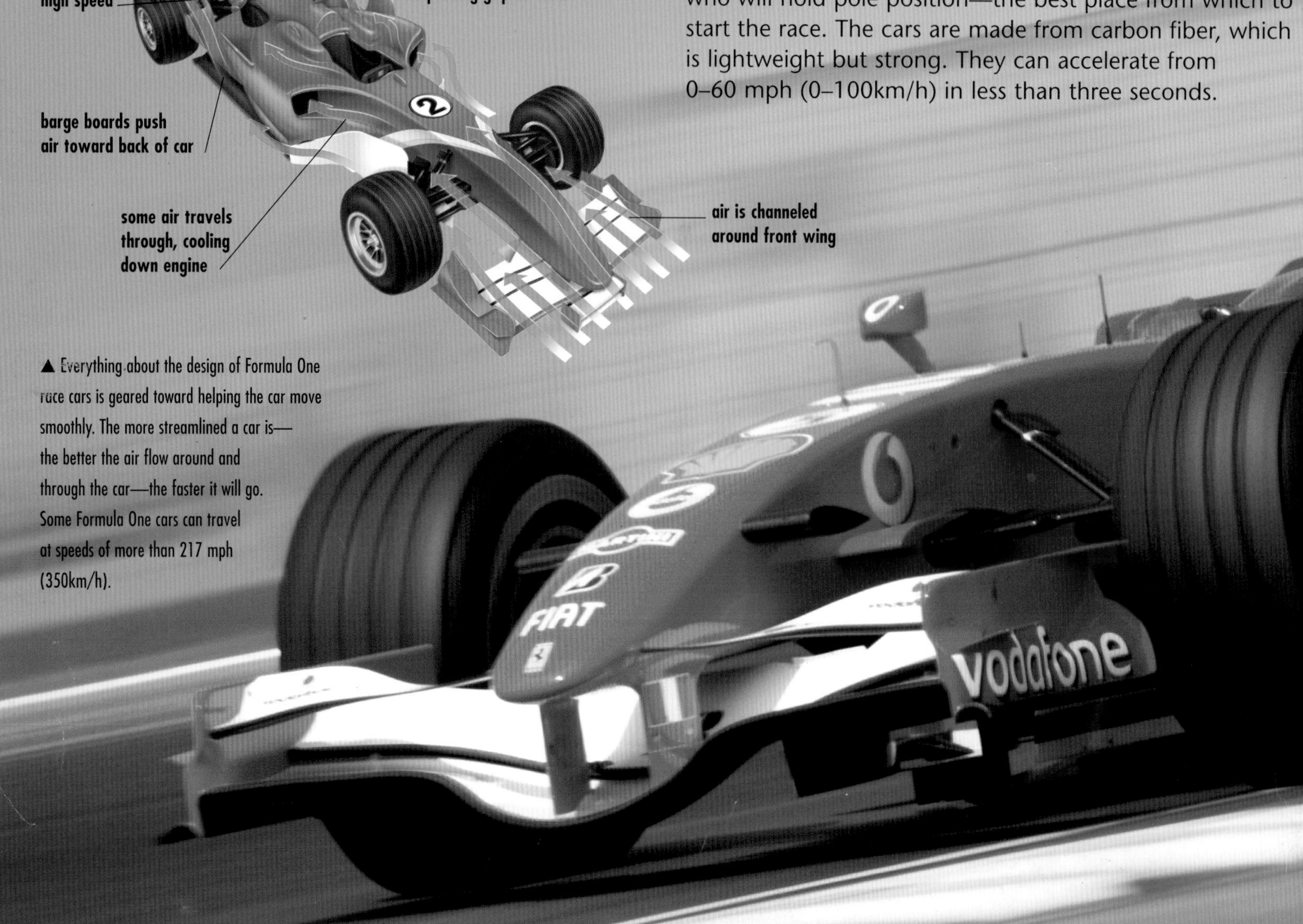
diffuser sucks out air from the back at high speed
like front wing and underbody, rear wing generates downforce, improving grip on road
barge boards push air toward back of car
some air travels through, cooling down engine
air is channeled around front wing
FIAT
vodafone

▲ Everything about the design of Formula One race cars is geared toward helping the car move smoothly. The more streamlined a car is—the better the air flow around and through the car—the faster it will go. Some Formula One cars can travel at speeds of more than 217 mph (350km/h).

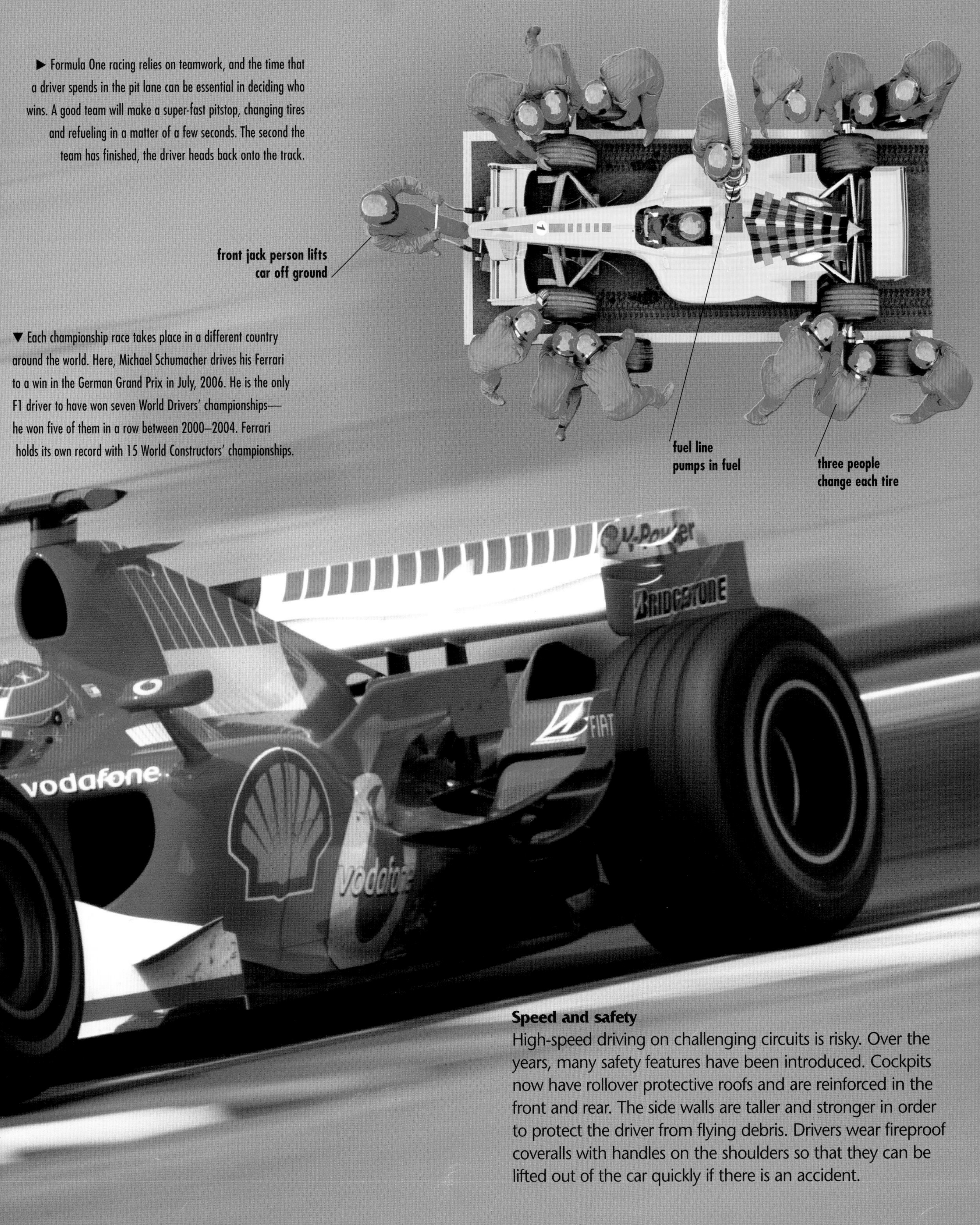
front jack person lifts car off ground
fuel line pumps in fuel
three people change each tire

► Formula One racing relies on teamwork, and the time that a driver spends in the pit lane can be essential in deciding who wins. A good team will make a super-fast pitstop, changing tires and refueling in a matter of a few seconds. The second the team has finished, the driver heads back onto the track.

▼ Each championship race takes place in a different country around the world. Here, Michael Schumacher drives his Ferrari to a win in the German Grand Prix in July, 2006. He is the only F1 driver to have won seven World Drivers' championships—he won five of them in a row between 2000–2004. Ferrari holds its own record with 15 World Constructors' championships.

Speed and safety

High-speed driving on challenging circuits is risky. Over the years, many safety features have been introduced. Cockpits now have rollover protective roofs and are reinforced in the front and rear. The side walls are taller and stronger in order to protect the driver from flying debris. Drivers wear fireproof coveralls with handles on the shoulders so that they can be lifted out of the car quickly if there is an accident.

Rallying

In March 1907, five cars set off from Peking (now Beijing), China to travel to Paris, France—a distance of 10,974 mi. (17,700km). The race took three months. In January 1911, the first Monte Carlo Rally took place. Twenty-three cars started from six cities around Europe; only 16 made it to Monte Carlo. These events marked the birth of international rallying—now a popular motorsport on many continents.

▶ Rallies are long-distance races that happen on public or private roads over several days or weeks and often through different countries. The driver and codriver travel in a series of stages over very rough terrain. The vehicles are usually specially adapted, like this Subaru Impreza WRC, which is being driven through Portugal by Petter Solberg of Norway in round six of the World Rally Championship in 2007.

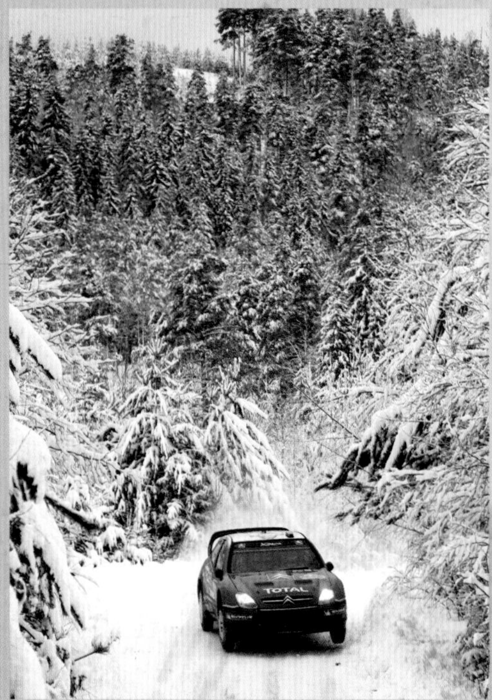

▲ Every February, one of only two rallies held on snow takes place in Sweden. Originally called the "Rally to the Midnight Sun," it became part of the World Rally Championship in 1973. This rally is usually won by Swedes and Finns, but in 2004, Frenchman Sébastien Loeb, with codriver Daniel Elena from Monaco, drove a Citroën Xsara to victory (above).

▶ Terrifying sandstorms, high dunes, rocks, and mud are among the many obstacles that face competitors in the grueling Dakar Rally. Here, France's Cyril Despres rides his KTM to victory during the seventh stage of the 2007 Dakar Rally between Zouerat and Atar in the western Sahara Desert.

The Dakar Rally

The first Dakar Rally ran from Paris, France down through Spain to Dakar, Senegal, on the west coast of Africa. The route varies each year, but it covers up to 9,300 mi. (15,000km) and usually ends in Dakar. It is an off-road endurance race with separate classes for bikes, cars, and trucks. The vehicles have to cross some very difficult mountainous and desert terrain.

The World Rally Championship

From 1973, this series of rallies has been run by the *Fédération Internationale de l'Automobile* (FIA), the international governing body for many motor-racing events. Every year, the series includes up to 16 rallies around the world. At the end of this series there is a winning driver and a champion manufacturer. In 2007, Sébastien Loeb of France won his fourth world championship in a row. In the same year, the manufacturer's prize went to Ford for the second year in a row.

Mountain movers

Some truly extraordinary working machines have been specially built to help with heavy tasks. Giant tunnel borers create road and railroad tunnels that travel under oceans and through mountains. Special dump trucks ferry loads of up to 380 tons (345 metric tons) at a time. Giant excavators help move actual mountains of earth and rocks in open-air mines.

▲ In the estuary of the Chiang Jiang (Yangtze River) near Shanghai, China, the largest tunneling machine in the world—the Double Shield TBM—is at work. It is being used to create two three-lane expressway tubes through clay, silt, and sand at a rate of 1,312 ft. (400m) per month.

▼ The Bagger 288 is used to clear earth and rocks from open-air sites in Germany so that coal can be mined. Its blade (inset) has 18 buckets that rotate, picking up earth and rocks at a rate of 33 ft. (10m) per minute before tipping this "overburden" onto a long conveyor belt that carries it away.

70.8-ft. (21.6-m)-wide bucket wheel excavates 2,500 truckloads per day
overburden travels along conveyor belts

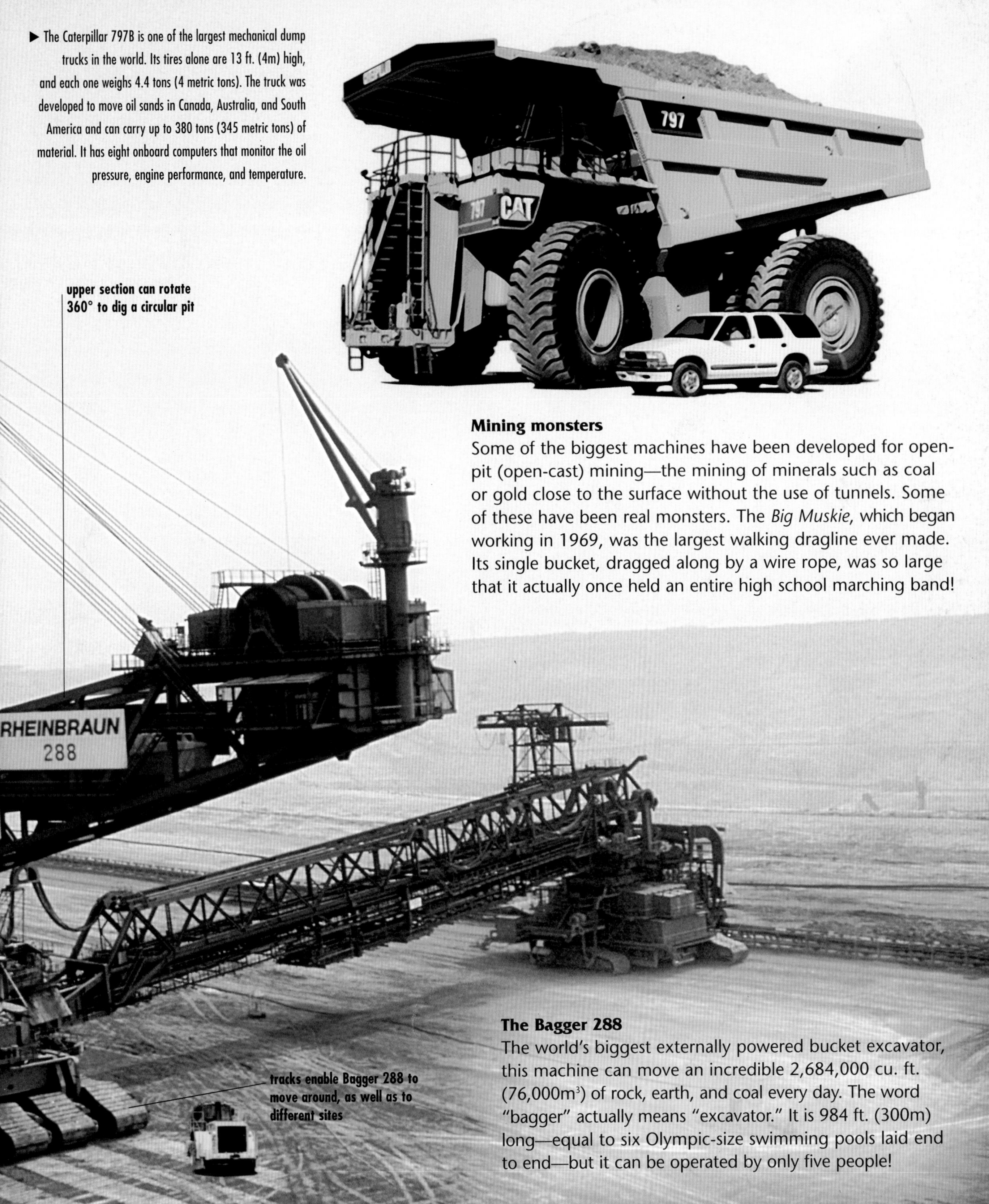
797
CAT
RHEINBRAUN
288
upper section can rotate 360° to dig a circular pit
tracks enable Bagger 288 to move around, as well as to different sites

▶ The Caterpillar 797B is one of the largest mechanical dump trucks in the world. Its tires alone are 13 ft. (4m) high, and each one weighs 4.4 tons (4 metric tons). The truck was developed to move oil sands in Canada, Australia, and South America and can carry up to 380 tons (345 metric tons) of material. It has eight onboard computers that monitor the oil pressure, engine performance, and temperature.

Mining monsters

Some of the biggest machines have been developed for open-pit (open-cast) mining—the mining of minerals such as coal or gold close to the surface without the use of tunnels. Some of these have been real monsters. The *Big Muskie*, which began working in 1969, was the largest walking dragline ever made. Its single bucket, dragged along by a wire rope, was so large that it actually once held an entire high school marching band!

The Bagger 288

The world's biggest externally powered bucket excavator, this machine can move an incredible 2,684,000 cu. ft. ($76,000m^3$) of rock, earth, and coal every day. The word "bagger" actually means "excavator." It is 984 ft. (300m) long—equal to six Olympic-size swimming pools laid end to end—but it can be operated by only five people!

Wheeled monsters

There are some truly monstrous trucks out there. A monster truck is a vehicle that has been built or modified so that it has very large wheels and suspension—the part that links the body to the wheels. These sports vehicles take part in competitions and displays that often include jumping over large obstacles. The first monster truck was *Bigfoot*, driven by American Bob Chandler in the 1970s.

▼ At 69.147 mph (111.527km/h), *Bigfoot 14* (seen below in competition) set the record for the fastest monster truck in 1999. In the same year, *Bigfoot 15* was the first monster truck to jump over a 727 aircraft, setting a world record for a long jump of 201.946 ft. (61.569m).

Safe monsters

There are many built-in safety features in the modern versions of monster trucks. Most have three kill switches—one of which is remotely controlled by an official race observer. The switches turn off the engine and electric components if there is an accident or rollover. Drivers sit in the center of the cab and are protected by a roll cage. They wear eye protection, neck collars, helmets, and fireproof suits.

▶ Until monster trucks came on the scene, traveling over obstacles and crushing them was something that was normally done only by tanks in war zones. This antiaircraft missile system's tracks can carry it over all types of terrain. The TOR-M1 is a transporter launcher vehicle (TLV) that is able to launch surface-to-air guided missiles.

Monster wheels

Monster trucks have lightweight bodies made of fiberglass over a tubular steel frame, supported by very large wheels. The wheels are the type made for heavy machinery such as fertilizer spreaders or other farm equipment. The trucks drive straight over all types of obstacles, especially rows of smaller cars, so the tires have to be extremely tough. They travel up and over the obstacles, crushing them as they go.

▲ To make sure that other monster trucks could not lay claim to being the largest, Bob Chandler put 10-ft. (3-m)-tall tires on *Bigfoot 4*. Then, in 1986, he built *Bigfoot 5* specifically to take these tires. Finally, in 2002, *Bigfoot 5* (above) was officially given the title of the "World's Tallest, Widest, and Heaviest Monster Truck."

▲ Before any rigs can run, a 347-mi. (560-km) ice highway has to be created across permafrost and frozen lakes. The Hagglund BV206 (above) is an incredible amphibious vehicle that is able to travel on any terrain. It exerts only half the ground pressure of a single human footprint and is used to mark a safe route on the thickest ice. It can even pull itself out if the ice cracks.

Ice road trucking

Ice road trucking is one of the world's most dangerous jobs. When the lakes of northern Canada freeze over in the winter, truckers have only two to three months to get one year's supply of equipment and food to the diamond mines northeast of the town of Yellowknife in the Northwest Territories. In freezing temperatures, their heavy 18-wheeler rigs carry huge loads along purpose-built frozen highways. If, for any reason, their engines stop or the ice cracks, the truckers will most likely die.

► An even surface on the ice roads is of vital importance for the truckers that travel along them. The ice constantly crackles and groans beneath the wheels of the heavy vehicles. To begin with, a team of snowplows sculpts the ice roads, scraping the snow to the side as they move along. Over the following months, they continue to maintain the roads, even drilling holes into the ice in order to flood it so that it refreezes and becomes thicker.

▲ The truckers are assigned their loads at the depot in the town of Yellowknife. They carry vital supplies along the Ingraham Trail (named after a local hero) to three main diamond mines. The most northern of these and the first to open—in 1998—was the Ekati Mine, which is only 124 mi. (200km) south of the Arctic Circle.

Supplying the mines

In 1991, diamond deposits were discovered in the Lac de Gras area of Canada. Today, the Canadian diamond industry is the third-largest in the world. The ice truckers can make one year's salary in just two months, so 600 truckers travel day and night in a race to get 10,000 loads to the mines before the ice melts.

Avoiding disaster

Although the truckers are under pressure to deliver their enormous loads, they cannot afford to make mistakes. They travel in temperatures as low as –67°F (–55°C) and endure Arctic snowstorms, whiteouts, and fog. If a fuel pipe freezes, the trucker may die from the cold. If a rig sinks, the driver has only one minute before they freeze to death. For these reasons, the rigs usually travel in convoys.

▶ When heavy rigs move over the ice, they create waves underneath. A wave can crash through the surface if the rig moves too fast onto the wave it has created. The wave will blow out in front of the speeding truck, causing the truck to fall into the water. The truckers must observe very strict speed limits, or they are banned from driving.

Amazing movers

Some extraordinary vehicles have been used to move around on land. Some are purpose-built to carry people over difficult terrain, while others move the heaviest of loads. Yet others are unique—the longest car ever built was a 26-wheeled Cadillac limousine named the *American Dream*, which was mainly used for movies and exhibitions. It was 100 ft. (30.5m) long and equipped with a king-size waterbed and a swimming pool complete with diving board!

USA
NASA
Atlantis
crawler weighs 2,993 tons (2,721 metric tons)
two control cabs on opposite corners allow crawler to be driven forward or backward without having to turn around

▶ The space shuttle *Atlantis* is moved to Launch Pad 39A in September 1996. The shuttle weighs 2,200 tons (2,000 metric tons), and the mobile launch platform weighs 4,609 tons (4,190 metric tons). Moving them is not easy. In order to do this, NASA has two crawler-transporters. They are the largest flatbed transporting machines in the world.

◀ Snowmobiles are built for endurance. They are used to travel on snow and ice and are able to cross most terrains, using tracks at the rear for driving and skis up front for steering. The longest snowmobile journey was 12,136.16 mi. (19,574.45km) in Canada and the U.S. It took 60 days between January and March 2008.

Moving houses

Houses, churches, and even lighthouses can be moved intact. On June 5, 1999, the 200-ft. (61-m)-tall Cape Hatteras lighthouse in North Carolina was moved inland, away from the threatening waters of the Atlantic Ocean that were moving closer. The lighthouse was lifted up by hydraulic jacks and steel rails placed under its base. Rollers were bolted to the rails, and five hydraulic rams pushed the load forward. It took 23 days for it to travel 2,886 ft. (880m).

▼ Prefabricated buildings are often moved from place to place. In some parts of the U.S., it is not unusual to see a truck moving along the highway with a two-story house balanced behind it. Here, housing for oil workers is being carried across the ice in northern Alaska.

Crawling along

Each one of NASA's two crawler-transporters at the Kennedy Space Center in Florida has 16 traction motors. The motors are powered by four generators driven by two diesel engines. The crawlers are 131 ft. (40m) wide and 115 ft. (35m) long. When carrying rockets and shuttles, they can reach a maximum speed of only 1 mph (1.6km/h). When they travel the 3.5 mi. (5.6km) from the vehicle assembly building to the launch pad, it takes around five hours.

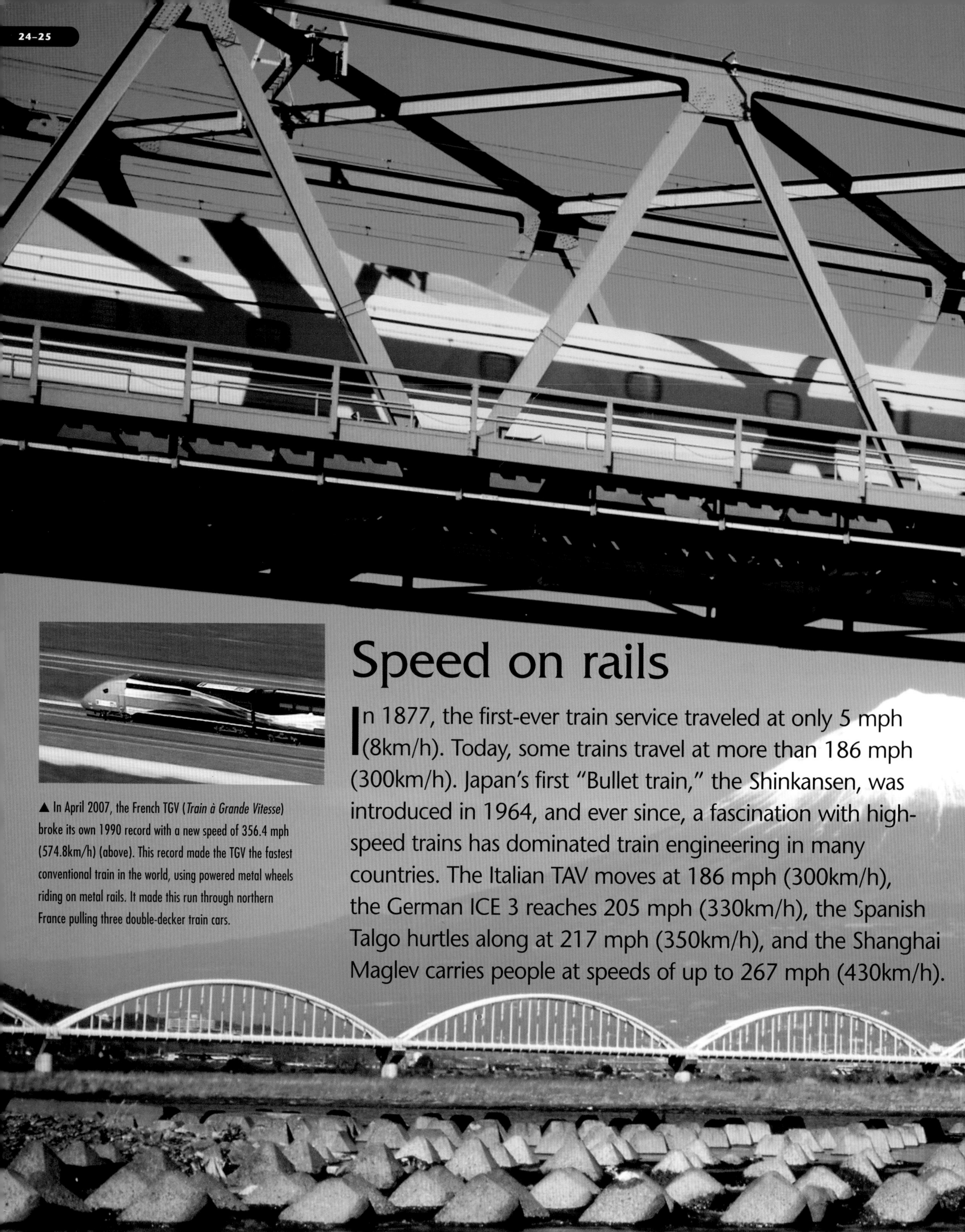

▲ In April 2007, the French TGV (*Train à Grande Vitesse*) broke its own 1990 record with a new speed of 356.4 mph (574.8km/h) (above). This record made the TGV the fastest conventional train in the world, using powered metal wheels riding on metal rails. It made this run through northern France pulling three double-decker train cars.

Speed on rails

In 1877, the first-ever train service traveled at only 5 mph (8km/h). Today, some trains travel at more than 186 mph (300km/h). Japan's first "Bullet train," the Shinkansen, was introduced in 1964, and ever since, a fascination with high-speed trains has dominated train engineering in many countries. The Italian TAV moves at 186 mph (300km/h), the German ICE 3 reaches 205 mph (330km/h), the Spanish Talgo hurtles along at 217 mph (350km/h), and the Shanghai Maglev carries people at speeds of up to 267 mph (430km/h).

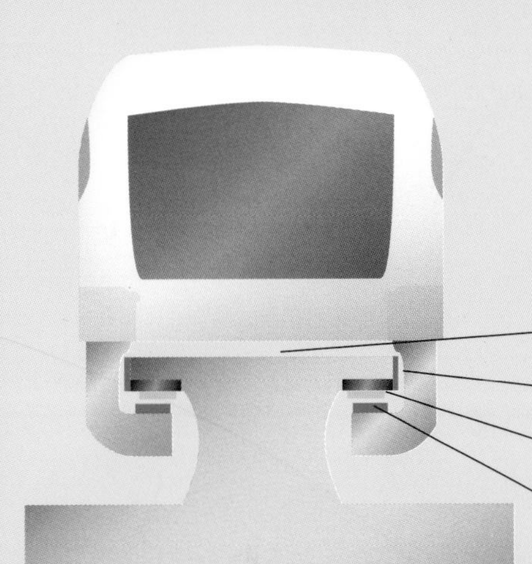

◀ The German ICE 3 maglev train (left) has electromagnets on each side along its entire length. They are attracted to iron rails under the edges of the guideway that the bottom of the train wraps around. This attraction levitates the train so that it floats around 0.4 in. (1cm) above the guideway. An electric current causes guide magnets to alternate, propelling the train forward.

▲ A Shinkansen train runs at an average speed of 162.3 mph (261.8km/h) along the Tokaido line with Mount Fuji in the background. "Shinkansen" means "new trunk line," but its popular name is *dangan ressha*, meaning "bullet train."

Traveling like a bullet

The super-high-speed Shinkansen travels at speeds of up to 186 mph (300km/h) on a network of tracks linking most of the main Japanese cities. This is the world's busiest high-speed railroad network, carrying 375,000 passengers a day. Rail technology is extremely important in Japan, a country that is densely populated and looking for ways to protect the environment. The Japanese government heavily promotes rail travel and discourages the use of cars.

The new technology

The Shanghai Maglev ("magnetic levitation") train is the world's first commercial high-speed maglev, achieving a world-record speed of 311 mph (501km/h). This Chinese-run train "floats" (see above), so it has no need for moving parts; it therefore needs little maintenance. It is almost silent when moving slowly and can move very fast because there is no friction. However, maglevs cannot run on existing tracks, only on special tracks that are very expensive to build.

Across the roof of the world

The highest railroad in the world is the line from Qinghai in China to Lhasa in Tibet, which travels across the north Tibetan plateau. The track goes through the Tanggula Pass at a dizzying height of 16,636 ft. (5,072m) above sea level. More than 595 mi. (960km) of track are higher than 13,120 ft. (4,000m), and extra oxygen is pumped into the train cars to prevent the crew and passengers suffering from altitude sickness.

Hauling freight

Across the world, freight trains are used to carry goods that people need from place to place. The trains travel on tracks that wind their way through the wildest of places—over high plateaus, through mountains, and under oceans. The freight is carried in containers, or open or covered wagons, depending on the goods and whether they need to be protected from the elements. Some goods need refrigerated containers, while liquids such as petroleum or chemicals travel in tanker wagons.

▲ Higher than the Peruvian railroad across the Andes, the Qinghai–Lhasa railroad crosses the high Kunlun and Tanggula mountain ranges. It carries freight and passengers across 341 mi. (550km) of permafrost. By transporting goods including minerals, agricultural products, and livestock by railroad instead of by road or ocean, costs have been reduced by around 75 percent.

▶ In remote places where there are few railroad lines, road trains are sometimes used to move bulky loads. A road train is a number of trailers that are pulled by one truck or heavy-duty vehicle. The longest was pulled 5 mi. (8km) by a Kenworth C501T truck near Kalgoorlie, Australia, in 2000. It was an incredible 3,339.7 ft. (1,018.2m) long and made up of 79 trailers weighing a total of 1,179.5 tons (1,072.3 metric tons).

Heavy goods

Some freight trains are able to move extraordinary loads. The longest freight train in the world—all 4,559 mi. (7,353km) of it—traveled across western Australia on June 21, 2001. Eight diesel-electric engines moved 682 wagons, loaded with 90,488 tons (82,262 metric tons) of ore, 170 mi. (275km) from the Newman and Yandi mines to Port Hedland. There was only one driver.

◀ In India, many trains carry both freight and passengers—and the passengers travel in or on the train in any way that they can. This train is carrying pilgrims on the way to a shrine. The Indian government runs the national railroad network, which is the world's largest network under one management. It transports more than two million tons of freight and 17 million passengers daily.

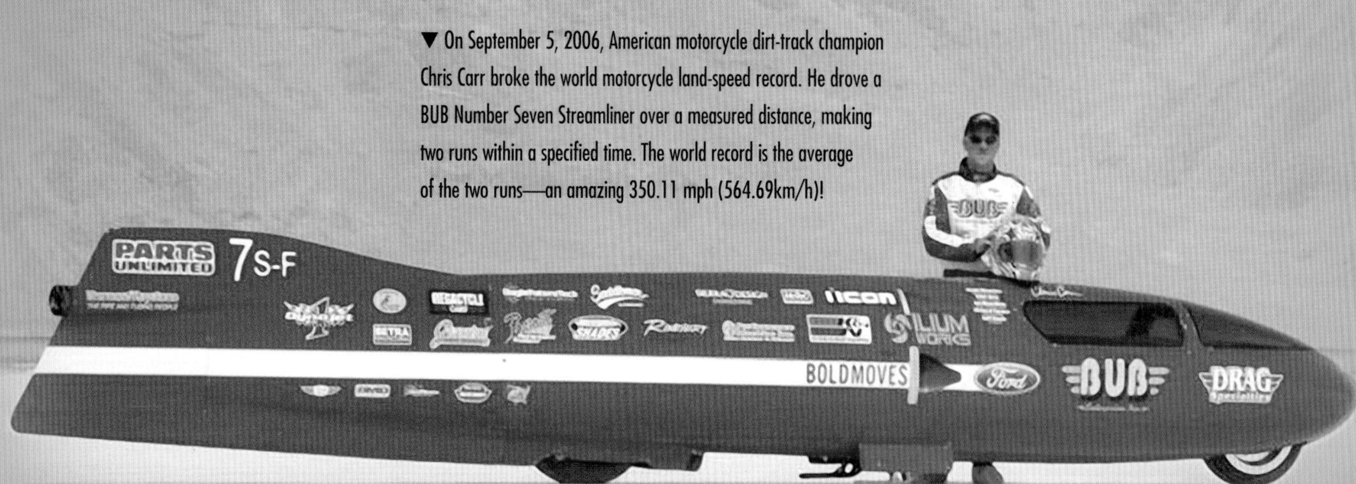

▼ On September 5, 2006, American motorcycle dirt-track champion Chris Carr broke the world motorcycle land-speed record. He drove a BUB Number Seven Streamliner over a measured distance, making two runs within a specified time. The world record is the average of the two runs—an amazing 350.11 mph (564.69km/h)!

On two wheels

Races on two wheels take place on roads, on racetracks, and off-road over all types of terrain. Bicycle races include cyclo-cross, mountain bike events, BMX races, and cycle speedway on dirt tracks. One of the earliest motorcycle races was the annual Isle of Man TT (Tourist Trophy), which began in 1907. Twenty-seven competitors did ten laps of a 15-mi (24-km) circuit on public roads. Today, as well as the TT, there are Grand Prix races and rallies and the grueling 24 hours of Le Mans Moto, a yearly endurance race.

◀ Fred Rompelberg rides his record-breaking bicycle to victory on October 3, 1995 on the Bonneville Salt Flats, near Salt Lake City, Utah. He earned his place in history by reaching an incredible 166.675 mph (268.831km/h), pedaling the bicycle behind a dragster to reduce wind resistance. The wheels had special lightweight aluminum rims, hubs, and spokes, and the whole bike weighed only 43 lbs. (19.5kg).

Pedal power

There are some true champions among cyclists. Dutchman Fred Rompelberg achieved no less than 11 world records for cycling behind heavy engines and is the holder of the Absolute Speed World Record for Cycling with a speed of almost 167 mph (270km/h) (above). American cyclist Lance Armstrong carved his name in cycling's history book as the only rider to have won the Tour de France seven times in a row (1999–2005).

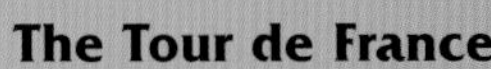

The Tour de France

Probably the most difficult bicycle race of all, the Tour de France, which began in 1903, is staged over three weeks every summer. Twenty teams of nine riders each travel 2,232 mi. (3,600km) across France and neighboring countries, finishing in Paris. There are time trials and stages, with flat plains and high mountains to cross. After each stage, successful cyclists are rewarded with different-colored shirts—yellow, green, polka dot, and white.

▲ In the 1990s, two Frenchmen, Christian Taillefer (above) and Eric Barone, battled to set a series of world records. Wearing rubber suits and aerodynamic helmets, they sped downhill on speed bikes in the French Alps. In 2007, Austrian Markus Stöckl smashed their records in the Chilean Alps with a speed of 130.5 mph (210.4km/h).

◀ American cyclist David Zabriskie rides in a time trial during the first stage of the 2005 Tour de France. Cyclists usually ride three different types of bicycles: one for time trials, one for flat road stages, and a lightweight bike for the mountainous stages. Zabriskie won this time trial, ahead of Lance Armstrong.

▲ In 1995, Emilio Scotto arrived home in Argentina at the end of the longest trip on a motorcycle. He had taken ten years to travel 455, 700 mi. (735,000km), visiting many countries, including China (above), on his black 1100 Honda Gold Wing, the "Black Princess." His book about these adventures, *The Longest Ride*, was published in 2007.

SUMMARY OF CHAPTER 1: LAND TRANSPORTATION

A fight to the finish
Between December 1898 and April 1899, the official land speed record was set and broken an amazing six times. There were only two men in the running, Camille Jenatzy of Belgium and Gaston de Chasseloup-Laubat of France. These rival racers each held the record three times—on one occasion for only a matter of hours! Camille Jenatzy was the first person to break the speed barrier of 60 mph (100km/h), doing so in his electric-powered vehicle, *La Jamais Contente* ("Never Satisfied"). On April 29, 1899, he reached 65.65 mph (105.88km/h) in Achères, France.

Salt-flat records
The Bonneville Salt Flats in Utah is more than 29,640 acres of land so barren that no life can exist there. It is named after the explorer Captain Benjamin Bonneville, whose employee and fur trapper Joseph Walker mapped and explored the area in the 1830s. In 1896, publisher William Randolph Hearst asked W. D. Rishel to find the shortest, fastest route for a cycle race. Rishel saw the potential for racing, and in 1914, he persuaded "Terrible" Teddy Tetzlaff to try for a speed record in a car on the flats. Tetzlaff set an unofficial record of 141.42 mph (228.09km/h) traveling across the open spaces in his Blitzen Benz. By 1949, the salt flats had become recognized as the world's premier venue for attempts at world land-speed records, whether for cars, trucks, or motorcycles.

Camille Jenatzy and his wife riding in *La Jamais Contente*

Go further . . .

Discover more about racecars and the organization that governs international races, the *Fédération Internationale de l'Automobile* (FIA): www.fia.com/en-GB/Pages/HomePage.aspx

Find out all the latest news about rallies around the world from the World Rally Championship (WRC): www.wrc.com

Learn all about the Japanese "bullet" train, the Shinkansen: http://english.jr-central.co.jp/index.html

Racing: The Ultimate Motorsports Encyclopedia by Clive Gifford (Kingfisher, 2006)

Constructor
A person or company that supervises the building of something such as a Formula One car.

Engineer
Someone trained and skilled in the design, construction, and use of engines and machines.

Racecar driver
A person who drives a vehicle in races for a living.

Researcher
Someone who studies a subject closely so that they can present it in a detailed and accurate way.

Discover the history of vehicles at:
The Henry Ford Museum
20900 Oakwood Blvd.
Dearborn, MI 48124
Phone: (313) 982-6001
www.thehenryford.org

Spend a day at the home of NASCAR:
Daytona International Speedway
1801 W. International Speedway Blvd.
Daytona Beach, FL 32114
Phone: (800) PIT-SHOP
www.daytonainternationalspeedway.com

Explore U.S. mass transportation history at the New York Transit Museum:
130 Livingston Street,
Brooklyn, NY 11201
Phone: (718) 694-3451
www.mta.info/mta/museum

Chapter 2

Water transportation

People who battle across oceans face some of the toughest challenges of all. They pit themselves against waves, tides, currents, and storms. Despite months of planning, they may find themselves in unpredicted danger. Many of the world's greatest yacht races—the Global Challenge, the Fastnet, and the Sydney to Hobart—end in disaster for some of the competitors. However, there are also triumphs; the world's best sailors push themselves to their limits to circumnavigate the globe on their own or bring their yacht safely into harbor ahead of the pack.

There are extraordinary craft on or in the water. One of the fastest, *Miss Budweiser*, skimmed along the surface of a lake at 219 mph (354km/h). Submersibles carry people to the deepest depths. Passengers can travel on cruise ships that are like entire cities on water.

Yachts reach the first marker point at the start of the Sydney to Hobart race, Australia, in December 2006.

▲ Donald Campbell set his final world speed record of 275.72 mph (444.71km/h) in *Bluebird K7* on December 31, 1964, on Coniston Water, in the United Kingdom. The last record that his father, Malcolm Campbell, had set was on the same stretch of water 25 years earlier. He reached 141.43 mph (228.11km/h) in *Bluebird K4* on August 19, 1939.

Water-speed records

Just after 8:30 A.M. on March 13, 2004, the hydroplane *Miss Budweiser* shattered all previous world records by reaching a speed of 220 mph (354.849km/h). Driven by Dave Villwock across Lake Oroville in California, it set an as yet unbeaten record for propeller-driven craft. However, this is not the fastest craft on the water. That record is still held by Ken Warby's jet-powered *Spirit of Australia,* with its 316.9 mph (511.13km/h) run in 1978.

▼ *Miss Budweiser* set the record for propeller-driven craft as it sped across Lake Oroville, in California, on the return leg of its two runs. The team that built *Miss Budweiser* is probably the most successful in hydroplane racing history. Between 1963 and 2002, its boats took part in 354 races, finishing in the top three 230 times with a record 134 victories. They also designed the enclosed cockpit.

A family business

In 1964, Englishman Donald Campbell set both water and land speed records in the same year—the only person ever to have done so. Between them, Donald and his father, Malcolm Campbell, set 11 speed records on water and 10 on land. They both drove boats and cars that they named *Bluebird*. Donald died on January 4, 1967, when *Bluebird K7* disintegrated at a speed in excess of 300 mph (480km/h).

▲ The *Spirit of Australia* flies along on its record-breaking run on October 8, 1978. The jet-powered hydroplane reached 316.9 mph (511.13km/h) on Blowering Dam in New South Wales, Australia. It smashed its own record of 287.54 mph (463.78km/h) that had been set in November 1977.

Do-it-yourself speed

Most of the extraordinary machines that have achieved world speed records on water are designed, built, and run by teams of people. However, the world's fastest speedboat, the *Spirit of Australia*, was built of balsa wood and fiberglass in the backyard of the man who set the record. Using a $69 military surplus jet engine, Ken Warby created the craft that was to make him the fastest man on water.

▲ A boat that is built purely for speed is the *Hydroptère*. This trimaran hydrofoil, which "flies" on water, was designed by French sailor Alain Thébault. It is 59 ft. (18m) long and has broken two world records. In April 2007, it traveled over one nautical mile (6,080.89 ft., or 1,853.93m) at 41.14 knots (47.24 mph, or 76.19km/h) in 86.7 seconds and 1,643.15 ft. (500.96m) at 44.81 knots (51.45 mph, or 82.98km/h) in 21.8 seconds.

Wind power

Some of the most thrilling watersport champions use a sailboard, powered by the wind, to travel across the surface of the water. The earliest sailboards date back to the late 1950s. In 1968, two Californians patented a design that they called the Windsurfer, and the name stuck. Kitesurfing first became popular in Hawaii during the late 1990s. Both sports combine the skills that are needed for sailing and surfing. The surfers rely on the wind to help them ride the ocean's biggest waves.

Incredible journey

Flávio Jardim and Diogo Guerreiro are Brazilian windsurfing champions and expert sailors. On May 17, 2004, they set out on a journey that took them straight into the record books. Fourteen months later, on July 18, 2005, they arrived in the north of Brazil, having windsurfed 5,034 mi. (8,120km) along the Brazilian coast. Their expedition was sponsored by an environmental education organization.

◀ Jardim and Guerreiro's journey took them from Chuí in the south of Brazil to Oiapoque in the north of the country. After five months, they had reached Rio de Janiero. As they traveled along the coast, they stopped off regularly at schools and colleges to talk about topics such as renewable energy and fishing.

◀ Ecosurfers Jardim and Guerreiro were both only 23 years old when they windsurfed their way into the record books. They traveled light on their surfboards, carrying only a digital camera, a cellular phone, and a few essentials in backpacks. They completed the entire journey without a team providing support for them on land.

Gaining speed

A sailboard consists of a board and a rig (a mast, boom, and sail). Sails vary in shape and size and are mounted on a universal joint that allows the rig to be tilted in any direction. This means that the surfer can steer the board without a rudder. There are also wave boards and freestyle boards that are smaller and lighter. These are easier to maneuver, and are used to do jumps, flips, and loops.

◀ A windsurfer rides a wave in Hawaii. In March 2008, French windsurfer Antoine Albeau set the record for the fastest windsurf, traveling at 49.09 knots (56.36 mph, or 90.91km/h) in a specially built canal at Saintes Maries de la Mer, in the south of France. The previous two records were set by Irishman Finian Maynard.

▲ In kitesurfing, a power kite pulls a rider through the water on a kiteboard. Englishwoman Andreya Wharry (above) is one of the world's best kitesurfers. She set a new world record in September 2005—the longest continuous kitesurf. She traveled from Cornwall, in southern England, to County Waterford, in southeast Ireland, a distance of 132.4 mi. (213.5km), in eight hours and six minutes.

Skimming the waves

International yacht racing has produced some extraordinary sailors, but none have been more impressive than Ellen MacArthur. On February 7, 2005, she sailed her 75-ft. (23-m) trimaran *B&Q* into the record books. She had achieved the fastest solo circumnavigation of the globe. On top of that, she had broken five other records, setting speed records to the equator, the Cape of Good Hope, Cape Leeuwin in Australia, Cape Horn, and back to the equator.

▲ Ellen MacArthur gets ready for her record-breaking trip. She completed the 27,287-mi. (44,012-km) journey in 71 days, 14 hours, 18 minutes, and 33 seconds, beating the previous record by more than 32 hours. Astonishingly, in January 2008 her record was beaten by Frenchman Francis Joyon, who set a new time of 57 days, 13 hours, 34 minutes, and six seconds in his trimaran *IDEC II*.

▲ The high-speed mega yacht *Millennium 140* is powered by two incredible diesel engines and has jet turbine booster engines that allow it to reach speeds of up to 80 mph (130km/h). It is the world's fastest fully equipped yacht and can sleep 10 passengers and a crew of eight. It is built with lightweight materials throughout, including a hull constructed from a special strong aluminum alloy.

Luxury travel

Mega yachts are yachts of more than 98 ft. (30m). Some mega yachts are the height of luxury but still move very fast. The world's fastest, *Millennium 140*, was designed and named for the James Bond movie, *The World Is Not Enough*, in which it starred. Packed into this 139-ft. (42.4-m)-long yacht are a sky lounge deck, grand salon, formal dining room, country kitchen, and master suite, complete with jacuzzi.

Competitive streak

Yacht racing involves a variety of sailboats, from dinghies to giant ocean racers. It can be either inshore or offshore. Inshore racing usually takes place within sight of land or from land to nearby islands. Offshore racing goes across open water and oceans and includes some of the most exciting and challenging races in the world—the Fastnet, Sydney to Hobart, Global Challenge, and Transpacific.

◀ The Australian yacht *Brindabella* participates in the 59th Sydney to Hobart yacht race in December 2003. This annual "Bluewater Classic" race began in 1945 with only nine runners. In the last decade, there have been as many as 371 competitors. The fastest race was run in one day, 18 hours, 40 minutes, and 10 seconds by *Wild Oats XI* in 2005.

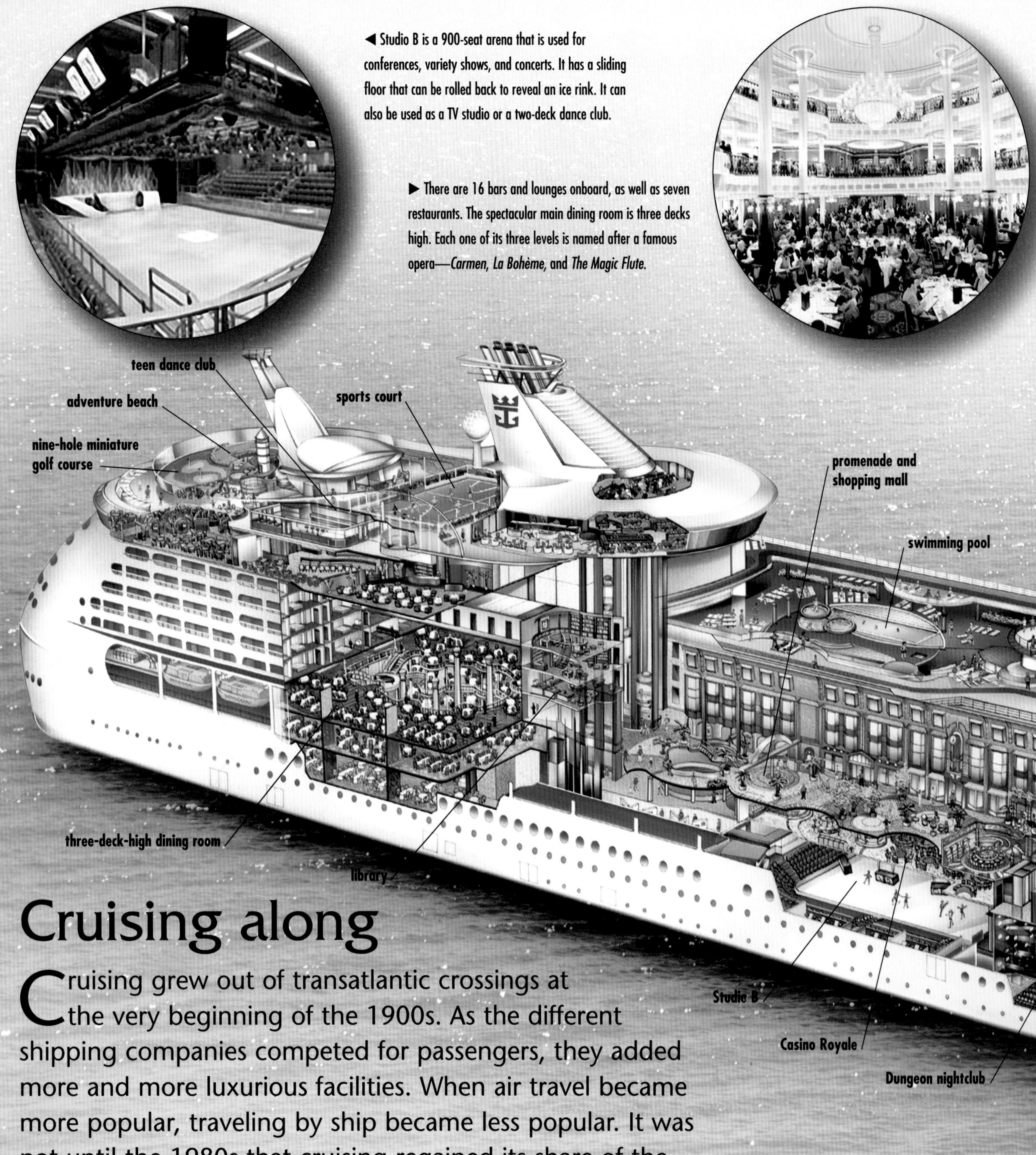

◀ Studio B is a 900-seat arena that is used for conferences, variety shows, and concerts. It has a sliding floor that can be rolled back to reveal an ice rink. It can also be used as a TV studio or a two-deck dance club.

▶ There are 16 bars and lounges onboard, as well as seven restaurants. The spectacular main dining room is three decks high. Each one of its three levels is named after a famous opera—*Carmen*, *La Bohème*, and *The Magic Flute*.

Cruising along

Cruising grew out of transatlantic crossings at the very beginning of the 1900s. As the different shipping companies competed for passengers, they added more and more luxurious facilities. When air travel became more popular, traveling by ship became less popular. It was not until the 1980s that cruising regained its share of the tourist industry. The *Voyager of the Seas*, at 137,276 gross tons, holds the record as the largest cruise liner of the last century.

First of its kind

When it was launched in 1999, the *Voyager of the Seas* was revolutionary—for its engineering and for the variety of onboard activities offered. It can carry up to 3,838 passengers and 1,181 crew. At 1,019.8 ft. (310.9m), it is almost as long as three soccer fields. It is 155.96 ft. (47.55m) wide, and its 14 decks rise more than 200 ft. (61m) above the waterline. Other ships built by Royal Caribbean since are even larger.

Floating resort

On this luxury liner, passengers are able to enjoy the first rock-climbing wall in the ocean, as well as a miniature golf course and driving range, a basketball court, and an inline skating track. There are swimming pools, whirlpools, a spa, and a large health and fitness club. There are even special provisions for the crew, who have their own deck complete with whirlpools, a gym, dining rooms, and a dance club.

▶ Through the center of the ship runs the Royal Promenade, a four-deck-high winding street. At two places along its length, there are atria (halls) that rise up 11 decks above the passengers' heads. The promenade is a shopping mall with stores, clubs, cafés, and bars.

▼ In the evenings, there is entertainment to suit all tastes. The Scala Theater (below) is five decks high and seats 1,350 people. It has a hydraulic orchestra pit and stage area, which can be raised and lowered. There is gambling in the Casino Royale, as well as a teen dance club, jazz club, and nightclub.

Across the oceans

There have been several incredible journeys across the oceans. On May 13, 1958, Australian Ben Carlin arrived in Montreal, Canada. It took him eight years to circumnavigate the globe in an amphibious jeep. He traveled 11,036 mi. (17,800km) across water and 38,936 mi. (62,800km) across land. When he set off in July 1950, he expected to travel across the Atlantic Ocean in only nine or ten days. Instead, it took 23 days because of a hurricane.

▲ Ben Carlin's jeep was called *Half-Safe* and was a modified vehicle from World War II. He began the journey with his new wife, Elinore, but she suffered from seasickness. When they reached India, she decided to jump ship, and he had a series of other shipmates for the rest of the voyage.

car is open underwater so exit is easy in an emergency
driver and passenger breathe compressed air from attached tank
salt-water resistant interior
zero emissions, so will not pollute
swissenergy
KGS VDO
SEABOB

▲ The *sQuba* submarine car has three electric motors that are powered by rechargeable lithium-ion batteries. One of the motors powers the back wheels on land. The other two motors power the propellers in the stern to push the car forward underwater. The *sQuba* dives to 33 ft. (10m) below the surface and can stay underwater for up to two hours.

▶ In Sydney Harbour on December 7, 2007, a 20-ft. (6.1-m) *Sealegs* craft became the fastest amphibious vehicle to travel 1,640 ft. (500m) on water, covering the distance in just 18 seconds. Two years before, in 2005, *Sealegs* almost halved the record time for the fastest crossing of the English Channel set by an *Aquada* driven by Richard Branson.

hydraulics raise and lower the front and back tires for land use

Driving underwater

Fifty years after *Half-Safe* completed its historic journey, another amphibious car hit the headlines. The world's first underwater car, the *sQuba* can be driven on land and underwater. Like the imaginary car driven by James Bond in *The Spy Who Loved Me* (1977), it is made from a Lotus sports car. It travels up to 74 mph (120km/h) on land, 4 mph (6km/h) on water, and 2 mph (3km/h) below the surface.

body panels are made of lightweight high-tech materials

Saving Earth

Traveling on or in water is always a major challenge and has inspired some revolutionary designs. One craft goes faster by actually submarining through the crests of the waves with its wave-piercing hull made of the heavy-duty material Kevlar. *Earthrace* (below) was built with environmentally friendly materials, is carbon neutral, and even has onboard recycling. It completed a record-breaking circumnavigation of the globe fueled with 100 percent renewable biodiesel.

▶ The futuristic trimaran *Earthrace* set out on its circumnavigation on April 27, 2008, from Sagunto, Spain, returning on June 27. The voyage took 60 days, 23 hours, and 49 minutes and knocked almost 14 days off the previous record set by *Ocean 7 Adventurer* in 1998.

Exploring the depths

Submersibles are small but very maneuverable. They are usually tethered to a support vessel, which means they have a relatively short range. They can be used to explore places that are normally impossible to reach. When the wreck of the *Titanic* was discovered on September 1, 1985, it was at a depth of 12,464 ft. (3,800m) off the coast of Newfoundland. One year later, a piloted deep-sea submersible named *Alvin* and an ROV (remotely operated vehicle) named *Jason Junior* were used to explore the wreck.

▼ *Alvin* may be the world's oldest research submersible, but it has been modified and updated several times. It can go as deep as 14,760 ft. (4,500m) during dives of 6 to 10 hours. Its six reversible thrusters allow it to maneuver or hover in one place. It is equipped with still and video cameras and has robotic arms to manipulate tools or collect samples.

Scientific explorer

Built in 1964, the U.S. Navy's Deep Submergence Vehicle *Alvin* was the world's first deep-sea submersible that was able to carry passengers. The pressure hull of the cockpit, which holds a team of three, is made of strong titanium. The life-support system can keep them alive for up to 72 hours if necessary. *Alvin* has been used to find hydrothermal vents and has helped find at least 300 new animal species.

▲ *Aluminaut* was the world's first submersible built out of aluminum. A deep-sea research vehicle, it helped recover *Alvin* from the Atlantic Ocean in 1969. The smaller submersible had become lost in 1968 when a cable snapped. The crew of three managed to escape, but *Alvin* sank in 4,920 ft. (1,500m) of water. One year later, the crew of *Aluminaut* managed to secure a line on *Alvin*, and the passenger-carrying robot was hauled up to the surface.

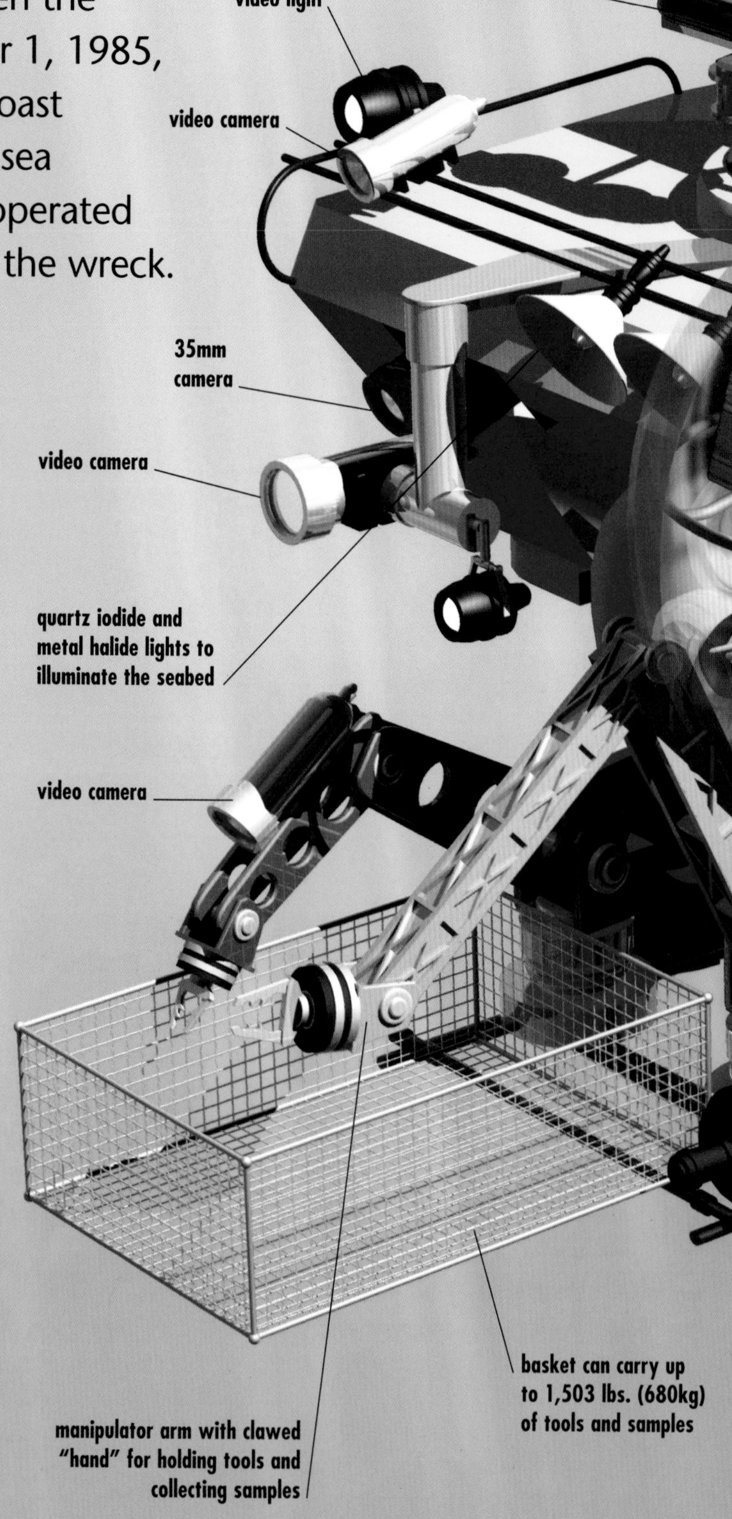

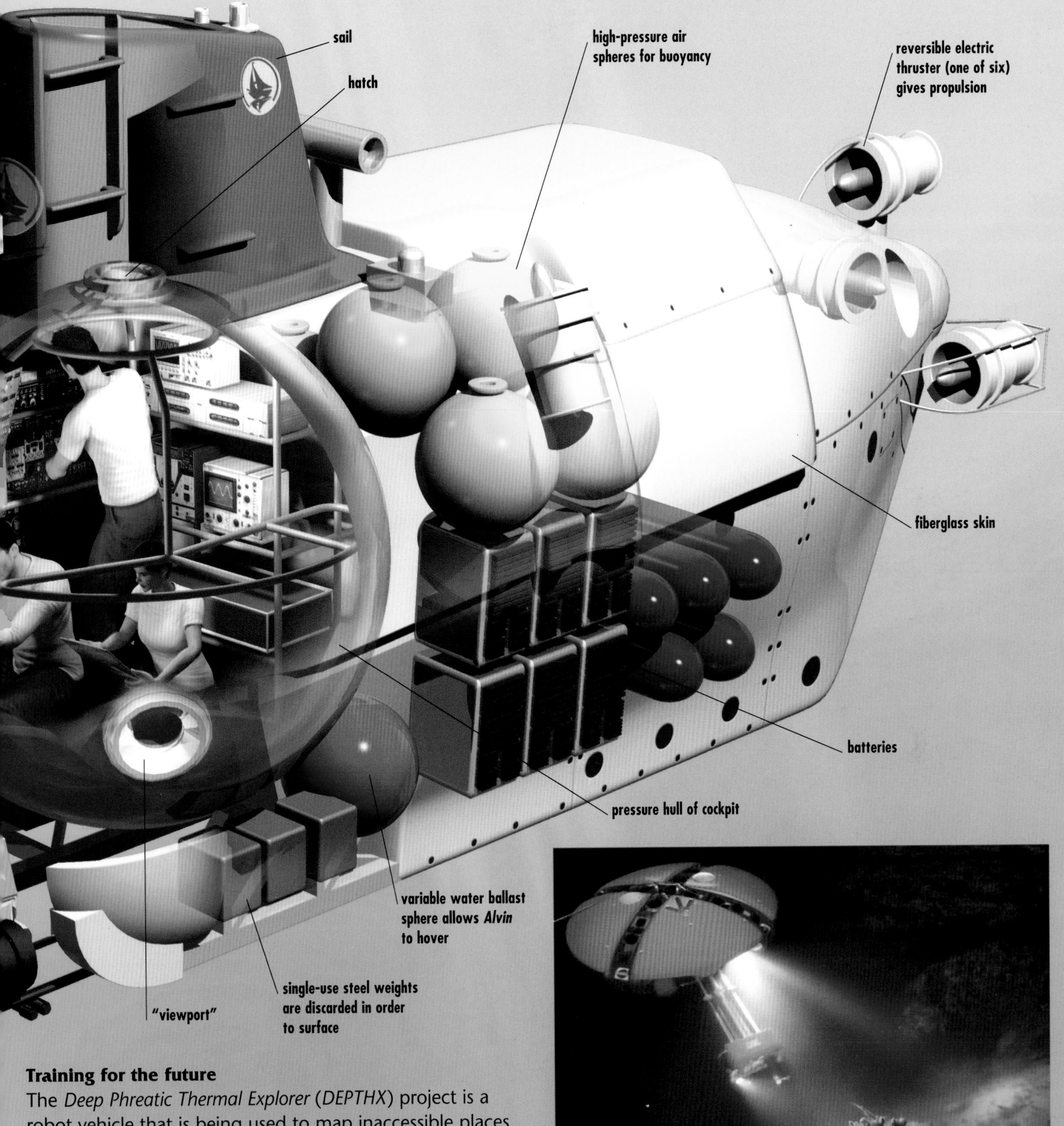

▲ *DEPTHX* is 8.2 ft. (2.5m) in diameter and weighs 3,300 lbs. (1,500kg). The robot is equipped with SLAM (simultaneous localization and mapping) technology, with which it created 3-D maps of El Zacatón's interior. On the way down the sinkhole, *DEPTHX* collected samples of water and materials from the walls. It discovered the previously unexplored bottom of the sinkhole, 1,043 ft. (318m) below the surface.

Training for the future

The *Deep Phreatic Thermal Explorer* (*DEPTHX*) project is a robot vehicle that is being used to map inaccessible places such as deep, flooded caverns. In May 2007, it reached the bottom of the world's deepest sinkhole, El Zacatón in Mexico. The NASA-funded robot is designed to search for life in Earth's extreme regions and maybe in the future on Jupiter's ice-covered moon, Europa.

SUMMARY OF CHAPTER 2: WATER TRANSPORTATION

Crossing the Atlantic Ocean

In 1838, the steamship *SS Sirius* traveled from Cork, Ireland, to Sandy Hook, New Jersey, in 18 days, 14 hours, and 22 minutes. This marked the beginning of ships competing to cross the Atlantic Ocean in the fastest time. In the 1860s, the transatlantic shipping companies created the Blue Riband prize. To begin with, the winners flew a blue pennant from their mast. Later, in 1935, a trophy was introduced. The prize is awarded for average speed during the journey, and there are separate prizes for eastward and westward crossings. Cunard's *Queen Mary* held the Blue Riband twice for crossing the ocean in both directions, in 1936 and 1938, and held this record until 1952.

The ships of tomorrow

People have always explored the world in boats, and boat building has progressed dramatically over the centuries. Small prehistoric coracles were made from animal skins stretched around a wooden frame, and ancient rafts were constructed from bundles of reeds. Today's ships are built for a specific purpose, whether they are sleek fiberglass racing yachts, steel-hulled battleships, or multihulled trimarans. In the future, new hull designs and efficient propulsion systems will enable sailors to go farther, and quicker, than ever before.

Tugboats guide the *Queen Mary* into the 51st Street Pier, New York City.

Go further . . .

Discover everything about the ocean and ships by visiting the U.K.'s National Maritime Museum: www.nmm.ac.uk/server/show/nav.3560

Find out the latest yachting news at Yachting World: www.yachtingworld.com/yw/home.htm

Learn all about *Alvin* and other submersibles: http://oceanexplorer.noaa.gov/technology/subs/subs.html

The New Complete Sailing Manual by Steve Sleight (Dorling Kindersley, 2005)

Windsurfing by Peter Hart (The Crowood Press, 2005)

Designer
Someone who creates plans for use in making something such as a ship.

Explorer
A person who travels into unknown or little-known regions to discover more about them.

Kitesurfer
A rider on a surfboard who is pulled through the water by a large kite.

Sailor
A person who works on a ship; any member of a ship's crew.

Windsurfer
Someone who rides on water using a special surfboard with a sail.

Discover maritime history:
San Francisco Maritime National Historic Park
Hyde St. Pier
San Francisco, CA 94123
Phone: (415) 447-5000
www.nps.gov/safr/

Explore the world of windsurfing with the U.S. Windsurfing Association:
PO Box 1261
Hood River, OR 97031
Phone: (877) 386-8708
www.uswindsurfing.org

Learn about maritime history at Chesapeake Bay Maritime Museum:
213 N. Talbot St., PO Box 636
St. Michaels, MD 21663
Phone: (410) 745-2916
www.cbmm.org

CHAPTER 3

Air transportation

Traveling through Earth's atmosphere is exhilarating. Hot-air balloons and airships float along, their canopies filled with low-density gas. Glider pilots search for thermal currents to lift them, silently spiraling higher. Passenger planes travel at 33,000 ft. (10,000m), carrying people from one side of the world to the other in less than a day. And paragliding, hang-gliding, and free fall parachuting are exciting sports for people who want to feel as if they are really flying like birds.

The fastest way for anyone to travel is by air, and the speediest planes are jets that travel several times faster than the speed of sound. The fastest aircraft of all was an unpiloted experimental NASA aircraft that, on November 16, 2004, reached almost Mach 10—10 times the speed of sound! In the future, this aerial technology may develop so that people are able to fly through space to the Moon or to nearby planets on regular scheduled flights.

The unpiloted X-43A scramjet-powered research aircraft traveled at Mach 9.6 (7,291 mph, or 11,760km/h) to set a world speed record.

Fastest in the air

The birth of the jet engine in the late 1930s changed aviation forever. Over the following decades, new engine designs made it possible to travel at ever-increasing speeds. The fastest aircraft of all are "supersonic," traveling faster than the speed of sound. They are mostly high-altitude, highly maneuverable reconnaissance aircraft. The only supersonic passenger plane was Concorde, which had a cruising speed of Mach 2.04 (1,364 mph, or 2,200km/h).

▶ The U.S. Air Force *SR-71 Blackbird* reconnaissance jet, built in the mid-1960s, remains the fastest piloted jet with a speed of more than three times the speed of sound. This supersonic jet's titanium skin resisted the heat generated at such a speed and protected the aluminum frame beneath. With side-facing radar and the ability to survey an area of 101,000 sq. mi. (260,000km^2), this extraordinary plane was also capable of avoiding missiles.

▲ The fastest combat jet is the Russian MiG-25 fighter, designed in the 1960s for high-altitude flight. It has been tracked traveling at about Mach 3.2 (2,105 mph, or 3,395km/h). The MiG-25 set 10 records while it was being tested, including speed over a 310-mi. (500-km) circuit, absolute altitude, and time to climb to an altitude of 98,400 ft. (30,000m).

Speeding in secrecy

Records for speed in the air are hard to establish. Usually, the jets concerned are developed for military use, so their speeds are not published. The world speed record is held by a MiG-25 (above) and was recorded by U.S. radar during a flight over Israel in 1973. It is known that the speed completely destroyed the engines. Afterward these planes could only travel safely at up to Mach 2.83 (1,860 mph, or 3,000km/h).

▶ The *Martin XP6M-1 SeaMaster*, which first flew in 1955, was the fastest flying boat ever built, with a top speed of 598 mph (965km/h). This U.S. Navy aircraft had an all-metal hull with sharply swept back wings. Its four turbojet engines were set on top of the wings to prevent them from being damaged by the water.

Flight of the *Blackbird*

From its first flight in 1964, the *SR-71 Blackbird* jet ruled the skies, flying top-secret missions for almost 25 years. It still holds the record as the fastest aircraft of all, with a top speed of Mach 3.3 (2,188.33 mph, or 3,529.56km/h). On its last flight on March 6, 1990, it set a record flying from Los Angeles to Washington, D.C. in one hour, four minutes, and 20 seconds at an average speed of 2,119 mph (3,418km/h).

The largest loads

The largest aircraft carry the largest loads, whether that be passengers or cargo. Often airliners are designed for either use—for example, the largest passenger airliner in the world, the Airbus A380, can also be set up to carry only cargo. Although the A380 carries the most passengers, it is not the largest and heaviest aircraft of all. That is the Ukrainian An-225 *Cossack*, designed to carry the Soviet space shuttle in 1988. It has a wingspan of 290 ft. (88.4m) and is 276 ft. (84m) long.

high-pressure hydraulic system to move rudders uses pump weighing 20 percent less than on other similar aircraft

◀ A Super Puma heavy-lift helicopter is unloaded from an Airbus A300-600 Super Transporter. The helicopter is 53.5 ft. (16.3m) in length and 15.1 ft. (4.6m) tall, and the Airbus has the capacity to carry two fully assembled helicopters with their blades folded. Cargo is lifted out through the upward-hinged main cargo door.

baggage containers in cargo hold on lower deck

economy-class seating on main deck

wingspan of 261.8 ft. (79.8m)

leading-edge flaps

dampeners on Rolls-Royce engines mean noise is half that of other jumbo jets

Super loaded

The Airbus A300-600 Super Transporter, nicknamed "Beluga," is one of the world's largest cargo carriers. Launched in 1994, it has the same wings, lower fuselage, undercarriage, and cockpit as the A300-600 passenger plane. The difference is that it is two stories high, longer than a basketball court, and is able to transport up to 52 tons (47 metric tons) of cargo. It is mostly used to carry large aircraft parts or even entire aircraft and helicopters.

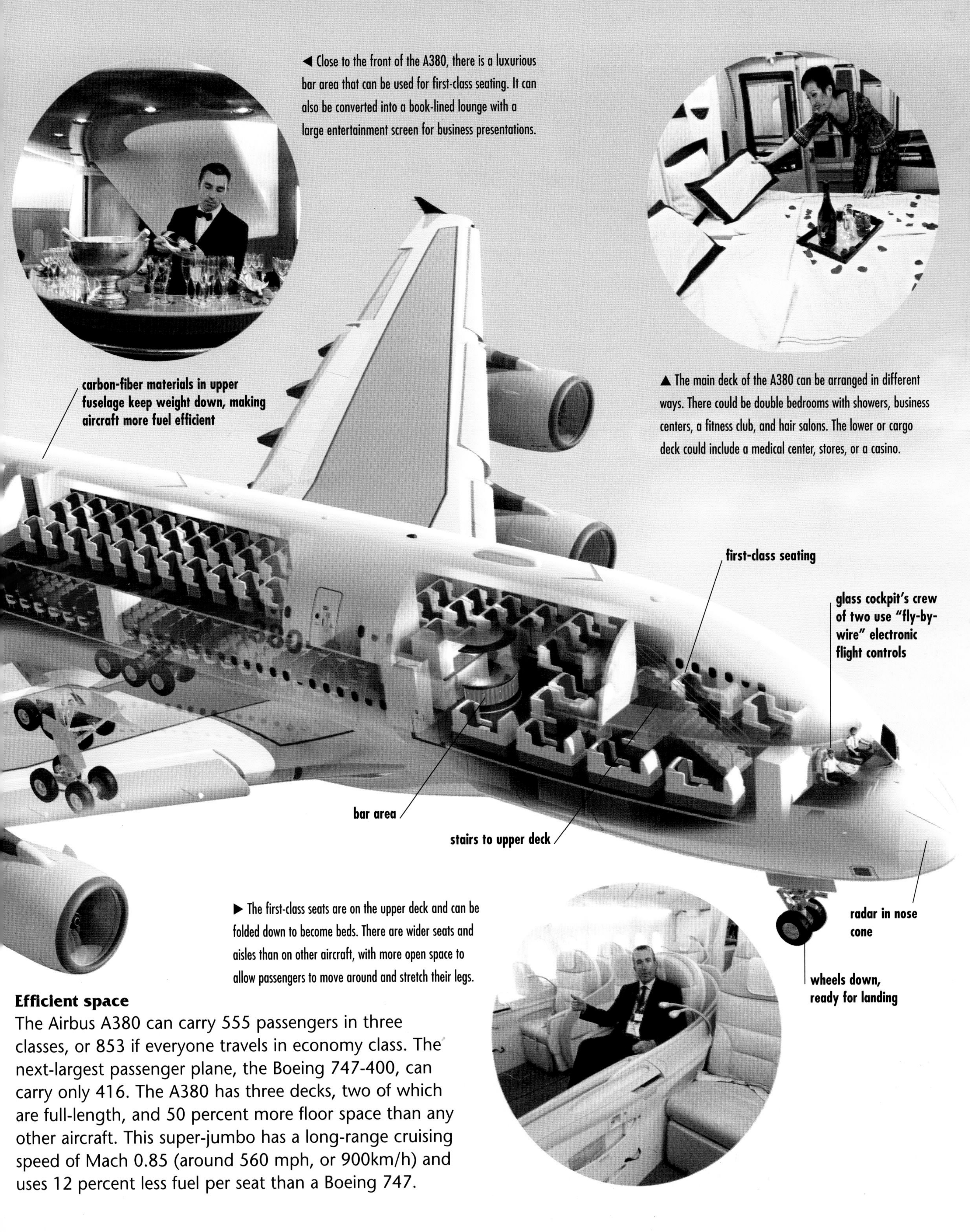
carbon-fiber materials in upper fuselage keep weight down, making aircraft more fuel efficient
first-class seating
glass cockpit's crew of two use "fly-by-wire" electronic flight controls
bar area
stairs to upper deck
radar in nose cone
wheels down, ready for landing

◀ Close to the front of the A380, there is a luxurious bar area that can be used for first-class seating. It can also be converted into a book-lined lounge with a large entertainment screen for business presentations.

▲ The main deck of the A380 can be arranged in different ways. There could be double bedrooms with showers, business centers, a fitness club, and hair salons. The lower or cargo deck could include a medical center, stores, or a casino.

▶ The first-class seats are on the upper deck and can be folded down to become beds. There are wider seats and aisles than on other aircraft, with more open space to allow passengers to move around and stretch their legs.

Efficient space

The Airbus A380 can carry 555 passengers in three classes, or 853 if everyone travels in economy class. The next-largest passenger plane, the Boeing 747-400, can carry only 416. The A380 has three decks, two of which are full-length, and 50 percent more floor space than any other aircraft. This super-jumbo has a long-range cruising speed of Mach 0.85 (around 560 mph, or 900km/h) and uses 12 percent less fuel per seat than a Boeing 747.

▼ The longest journey ever made by a powered paraglider was by American Bob Holloway in 2004. Between June 18 and July 12, he traveled 2,573 mi. (4,150km) from Astoria, Oregon to Washington, Missouri, following the trail of early 19th-century explorers Meriwether Lewis and William Clark.

Hanging in the air
Gliding takes many forms. In hang-gliding, the pilot lies facing downward in a harness hanging from a lightweight metal "V"-shaped framework that supports a fabric wing. Paragliders sit in a harness that also hangs from a fabric wing. The wing's crescent shape is formed only by the pressure of air entering through vents in the front.

Gliding and paragliding

In A.D. 852, the inventor Abbas Ibn Firnas jumped from the minaret of a mosque in Córdoba, Spain. He survived because he had used a large cloak like a parachute. Inspired by this, he built a glider that he tried to fly from the nearby Mount of the Bride. Unfortunately, he crashed, but over the following centuries many other people tried to follow his lead. Ibn Firnas controlled his glider by moving his body, just like pilots do in hang-gliders today.

▲ Paragliders launch themselves by running either over a cliff or down a slope. They can travel great distances. In July 2006, Aljaz Valic of Slovenia achieved the "out-and-return" world record of 161 mi. (259.7km) in Slovenia. In November 2007, three Brazilian pilots, Marcelo Prieto, Rafael Saladini, and Frank Brown, flew 286.3 mi. (461.8km) to earn the world straight distance record.

Flying high

Gliders can stay aloft for hours. They find the updrafts of warm air from Earth's surface, called thermal currents, and circle in them at altitudes of up to 9,800 ft. (3,000m). They also use ridge lift, when wind blows against the face of a hill and is forced upward. Wave lift—waves in the atmosphere that are like ripples on water—helped lift Steve Fossett and Einar Enevoldson into the stratosphere and set the world glider altitude record of 50,666 ft. (15,447m) in Argentina in 2006.

▲ On December 19, 2007, Laszlo Hegedus of Hungary set a world speed record over a triangular course. He flew 775 mi. (1,250km) at an average speed of 93.9 mph (151.5km/h) in Bitterwasser, Namibia. His glider was the elegant Schempp-Hirth Nimbus 4T (above). Pamela Kurstjens-Hawkins of the United Kingdom holds three speed and three distance gliding world records, all achieved when flying a Nimbus 4T.

Highest, longest, farthest

At 8:05 A.M. on Monday, February 1, 1999, *Breitling Orbiter 3* took off from the grounds of Château d'Oex in the Swiss Alps. On March 21, it touched down in the Egyptian desert after completing the first successful nonstop circumnavigation of the globe by balloon. Onboard were the pilots Bertrand Piccard and Brian Jones. They traveled 28,368 mi. (45,755km) in a flight lasting 19 days, 21 hours, and 55 minutes.

▲ Swiss psychiatrist and balloonist Bertrand Piccard waves to the 5,000-strong crowd that gathered to see the *Breitling Orbiter 3* take off. Balloonist Brian Jones, from England, was his copilot on this history-making flight. Piccard had failed with his first two attempts in *Orbiter* in 1997 and *Orbiter 2* in 1998.

◀ Satellite-based systems in the forward cockpit of the gondola were used to communicate with the control team on the ground. The control team used two GPS systems to track the balloon's route in real time and calculate the best altitude at which the pilots should fly.

Up, up, and away

Piccard and Jones broke distance, time, and endurance world records with their flight. For seven weeks, they traveled at altitudes of up to 37,303 ft. (11,373m) and were driven by jet-stream winds at speeds of up to 198 mph (320km/h). At one point, Piccard actually climbed out of the gondola to chip icicles off the balloon with a pickax! Along the sides of the gondola that hung beneath *Breitling Orbiter 3* were 32 titanium cylinders that fueled the balloon's six burners.

Living space

The gondola in which the two men traveled was 17.7 ft. (5.4m) long and made of a mixture of Kevlar and carbon fiber material. Solar panels under the gondola recharged batteries onboard to provide electrical power, and burners kept the temperature at a constant 59°F (15°C) for most of the time. There was one bunk in the center and a well-designed pressure-operated toilet in the rear. The two men lived mostly on rehydrated meals. They followed a strict rotation of eight hours at the controls, eight hours working with one another, and eight hours sleeping in the bunk.

◀ When fully inflated, the balloon was 180 ft. (55m) tall. It was made of a nylon fabric that was welded to a special helium-tight membrane. This was then covered in a skin coated with aluminum to give good temperature control. The gondola was 10.2 ft. (3.1m) high and weighed 4,400 lbs. (2,000kg).

Strange but true

During the last 100 years, some of the most extraordinary flying machines have been built. Some have been so huge that it is a wonder they were able to stay aloft. Others have set, broken, and held records for more than 50 years. Flying boats and airships, used for transportation, have been at the heart of great successes and dire disasters. People have constantly tested their own abilities to the limit in an effort to develop new ways to fly.

Winged wonder

On November 2, 1947, the *Hughes H-4 Hercules*, the largest flying boat ever built, made its first and only flight. Named the "Spruce Goose" by its critics, it was 218.5 ft. (66.6m) long and held the record as the largest plane in the world for many years. It still holds the record for the largest wingspan at 319.93 ft. (97.54m). The *H-4 Hercules* was built entirely out of wood by a team of engineers led by the eccentric American multimillionaire Howard Hughes.

▼ With Howard Hughes at the controls, the Spruce Goose glided over a 3-mi. (5-km) stretch of water in Long Beach, California. It reached 90 mph (145km/h), but it only achieved an altitude of 69 ft. (21m) for one minute. Afterward, Hughes had the flying boat put in a hangar and kept in good flying condition until he died in 1976.

Gas-filled giants

For many years, the German-built zeppelin airships ruled the skies. A zeppelin had a rigid internal metal skeleton that contained gas-filled bags, giving the craft lift. Built into the base was a compartment for the passengers and crew. When the *Hindenburg* was launched in March 1936, it was the largest airship ever built. It was 804 ft. (245m) long and had a maximum speed of 84 mph (135km/h).

▲ The *LZ-127 Graf Zeppelin* flies over London, England in 1931. The airship operated from 1928 to 1937. During this time it flew 590 flights and more than 0.93 million mi. (1.5 million km). In 1929, while circumnavigating the globe, the *Graf Zeppelin* crossed from Japan to San Francisco, California—the first nonstop flight of any aircraft across the Pacific Ocean.

◀ At 7:25 P.M. on May 6, 1937, the *Hindenburg* burst into flames as it came in to land in Lakehurst, New Jersey. A spark caused the rear section of the hydrogen-filled zeppelin to catch on fire as the airship was being secured to a mooring tower. In only 37 seconds, the airship was completely destroyed. Despite the intensity of the flames, 62 of the 97 passengers and crew onboard survived.

▶ On August 16, 1960, wearing a pressurized suit, American Joseph Kittinger jumped out of the gondola of a helium balloon, *Excelsior III*, at 102,772 ft. (31,333m). His records for the highest balloon ascent, the highest parachute jump, the longest parachute free fall (four minutes and 36 seconds), and the fastest speed by a human through the atmosphere (up to 613 mph, or 988km/h) still stand.

◀ The *ATV Jules Verne*, launched in March 2008, is a 22.8-ton (20.7–metric ton) cargo ship designed by the European Space Agency (ESA). It will deliver up to 8.4 tons (7.6 metric tons) of cargo to the International Space Station (ISS) and take away up to 7.2 tons (6.5 metric tons) of waste. The first one of a planned fleet, it is the first-ever completely automated space cargo ship and is capable of reboosting the ISS into a higher orbit.

Into space

Carrying cargo and passengers into space is big business in more ways than one. The vehicles used are probably the most expensive built on Earth, and they carry some of the largest loads. These transporters have included the Russian Progress M-53 freighter, the Space Shuttle orbiters, and the new Automated Transfer Vehicle (ATV). They have carried materials to build space stations and supplies and fuel for the crews who stay on them. They have also launched satellites and brought them back to Earth.

◀ Trainee astronauts take a ride in a specially adapted plane called the "Vomit Comet." It takes an arced flight path called a parabola. For 25 seconds, the plane falls away from the passengers at exactly the same speed that they fall toward it. They float in midair, as they would without gravity in space.

▲ Russian cosmonaut Valeriy Polyakov looks out through a porthole onboard the Soviet space station Mir. Polyakov holds the record for the longest space flight in history. He spent 438 days in space between January 1994 and March 1995. Mir was the first continuously inhabited research space station. It took 10 years to build and was in orbit for 15 years.

Building in space

The construction of the International Space Station (ISS) began in 1998, and it is still being assembled 217 mi. (350km) above Earth's surface. It travels at an average speed of 4.8 mps (7.7km/sec) and orbits Earth 15.75 times per day. The space station is a joint project by the space agencies of the U.S., Russia, Japan, Canada, and Europe. Materials to build the ISS are carried up into space by shuttles and the ATV.

Shuttle service

There are currently three space shuttles in the NASA fleet—*Atlantic, Endeavor,* and *Discovery*. There were originally five, but *Challenger* disintegrated 73 seconds after launch in 1986, and *Columbia* broke apart during reentry into Earth's atmosphere in 2003. The shuttles look like aircraft with their double-delta wings and carry astronauts and payloads to satellites and space stations. They are launched as rockets into orbit around Earth and land like gliders after reentry.

▼ The Space Shuttle *Discovery* approaches the ISS to dock. This shuttle has flown more flights than any other spacecraft. Like the other shuttles, it has a large payload bay (15.1 x 60 ft., or 4.6 x 18.3m), from which it launched the Hubble Space Telescope in April 1990 .

SUMMARY OF CHAPTER 3: AIR TRANSPORTATION

Reaching the skies
Over the centuries, many people have tried to fly. In 1783, the French Montgolfier brothers filled a huge paper balloon with hot air, and it rose into the air carrying two men. Almost 50 years later, Henri Giffard invented the first dirigible, or steerable balloon. In 1853, Sir George Cayley built a full-size glider, which is said to have carried his coachman across a valley. But it was in December 1903, in Kitty Hawk, North Carolina, that Orville and Wilbur Wright flew their gasoline-engined flying machine, the *Flyer*, for 131 ft. (40m). Real air travel had begun.

Transatlantic triumph
In April 1913, the United Kingdom's *Daily Mail* newspaper offered a prize of £10,000 to the first person to make a nonstop flight from North America to Great Britain or Ireland. Two months later, on June 14, British fliers John Alcock and Arthur Whitten Brown took off from Lester's Field in Saint John's, Newfoundland (now part of Canada), in a twin-engined Vickers Vimy IV. Alcock piloted and Brown navigated, and despite engine trouble and bad weather—at one point snow filled the cockpit—they landed in Clifden, western Ireland. Thinking that they had chosen a green field for their landing, they actually came down in a bog on Derrygimla Moor. They had traveled 1,885 mi. (3,040km) in just over 16 hours and were the first people to fly nonstop across the Atlantic Ocean.

Alcock and Brown's landing damaged the aircraft, but they were not hurt.

Go further . . .

Find out about learning to hang-glide or paraglide from the U.S. Hang Gliding and Paragliding Association: www.ushpa.aero

Discover where to see air shows in the U.S.: www.airshows.com

Flying Machine by Andrew Nahum (Dorling Kindersley, 2004)

Ultimate Thrill Sports: Hang Gliding by Noel Whittall (Gareth Stevens Publishing, 2007)

Balloonist
Someone who flies or rides in a balloon as a sport or hobby.

Cosmonaut
A Russian or Soviet astronaut—a person trained to travel in a spacecraft.

Inventor
Someone who thinks of or creates something for the first time.

Paraglider
Someone who travels from a height through the air wearing a wide, steerable parachute.

Pilot
A person qualified to fly a plane, balloon, or other aircraft.

Discover more about air and space travel and see the Wright brothers' flying machine and the *Apollo 11* command module at:
Smithsonian Air and Space Museum
Independence Ave. at 6th St., SW
Washington, D.C. 20560
Phone: (202) 633-2494
www.nasm.si.edu

See an air display by the Blue Angels, the Navy flight-demonstration squad, at various U.S. locations and visit the Museum of Naval Aviation:
1750 Radford Blvd.
Naval Air Station Pensacola, FL 32508
Phone: (850) 452-3604
www.blueangels.navy.mil/index.htm
(for details of air displays near you)

Glossary

acceleration
An increase in the speed of a moving object.

air resistance
The force that resists the movement of an object through the air.

alloy
A mixture of two or more metals or a mixture of a metal and a nonmetal.

altitude
The height of an object above sea level or above Earth's surface.

amphibious
Something (e.g. a vehicle) capable of operating on both land and water.

biodiesel
Vegetable oil and animal fat that is converted into fuel for heating systems and diesel engines.

carbon fiber
A strong, lightweight material made of almost pure carbon, used in the construction of aircraft and spacecraft.

carbon neutral
Giving off zero carbon dioxide into the atmosphere. Something is carbon neutral if either it gives off no carbon dioxide at all or if it gives off no more carbon dioxide than it absorbs.

centrifuge
A machine that spins around at high speed, used to test the effects of acceleration and deceleration on astronauts and pilots.

circumnavigation
To go completely around something, for example, Earth.

cosmonaut
A Russian or Soviet who is trained to participate in the flight of a spacecraft.

cyclo-cross
A bicycle race over a cross-country course that can require the rider to carry the bicycle over obstacles.

deceleration
A decrease in the speed of something.

density
A measure of how tightly packed the mass is in a substance.

double delta
The wing of an aircraft in the form of two triangles.

downforce
The downward pressure created by a car that allows it to travel faster by improving its grip on the track or road.

drag
The force that slows an object down as it travels through a liquid or gas.

drag racing
A race between cars to see which one can accelerate fastest from a standstill.

dragster
A car specially built or modified for drag racing.

emissions
Substances discharged into the air from an engine.

endurance
The ability to continue or last.

excavator
A machine used for digging and moving soil, sand, or gravel.

Two trucks move a family house in the United States

fiberglass
A plastic material reinforced with fine threadlike pieces of glass.

flatbed
A truck or trailer that has an open back with no sides and is used to transport large objects.

"fly-by-wire"
A semiautomatic, computerized flight control used for flying aircraft or spacecraft.

free fall
Describes the initial fall through the air by parachutists before they deploy their parachute.

freight
Goods or cargo carried from place to place by water, land, or air.

fuselage
The central part of an aircraft to which the wings and tail are attached.

g-force
The force acting on an object as a result of acceleration or gravity.

geothermal
Describes the energy harnessed from hot rocks inside Earth.

hydraulic
Describes a machine that is made to operate by a fluid under pressure.

hydrofoil
A speedboat with winglike structures attached to its hull, which lift it so that it skims over the water at high speed.

hydroplane
A high-powered boat designed to travel along the surface of the water at high speed.

hydrothermal vent
An opening in the seabed from which hot mineral-rich water flows.

SR-71 Blackbird

Francis Joyon's trimaran *IDEC II,* in which he beat Ellen MacArthur's solo around-the-world record in January 2008

jet engine
An engine that produces a stream of hot gas to propel a vehicle forward.

jet stream
Strong winds that circle Earth around 6 mi. (10km) above the surface.

Kevlar
A lightweight but very strong material used for many items, including tires, ropes, and sails.

lift
The upward force, produced by wings, that keeps an aircraft in the air.

Mach
A measurement of speed in relation to the speed of sound. Mach 1 is the same as the speed of sound. The speed of sound is around 745 mph (1,200km/h) at sea level, but it varies with the temperature, humidity, and pressure of the air.

orbiter
A spacecraft, planet, or satellite that orbits another body such as Earth.

permafrost
Ground that is permanently frozen.

prefabricated
Manufactured in sections for quick assembly.

pressure hull
The pressure-resistant hull of a submersible.

pressurized
At an atmospheric pressure that is higher than that of the surroundings.

reconnaissance
An inspection of an area, especially to collect military information.

renewable energy
A naturally occurring form of energy, such as wind, solar, or wave power, that is, in theory, inexhaustible.

rig
A large vehicle or truck.

roll cage
A metal cage fitted around the seat of a racecar to prevent the driver from being crushed if the car rolls over.

rudder
A movable blade at the stern of a boat or aircraft that can be turned in order to change direction.

satellite
An object that orbits a larger object. Artificial satellites orbit Earth and provide telecommunication links and information about Earth's surface. Natural satellites include the Moon, which orbits Earth.

sinkhole
A depression in the surface of land, usually in limestone areas, formed by the collapse of the roof of a cavern.

sonic barrier
The sudden increase in air resistance that happens to an aircraft as it approaches the speed of sound.

speedway
A road or track where high-speed driving is allowed.

Michael Schumacher's Ferrari F248 F1 car

stratosphere
The part of the atmosphere from 9–30 mi. (15–50km) above Earth's surface.

submersible
Any vessel capable of operating or remaining under the water.

supersonic
Faster than the speed of sound.

time trial
A race in which the competitors are timed individually on a set distance over a course.

titanium
A strong, corrosion-resistant metallic element used as an alloy for aircraft.

trimaran
A fast boat with three parallel hulls.

turbine
An engine in which a moving fluid, such as steam, water, hot gases, or air, is converted into mechanical power.

turbojet
A jet engine that is powered by a turbine.

whiteout
The complete loss of visibility because of snow or fog.

Index

Acknowledgments

The publisher would like to thank the following for permission to reproduce their material. Every care has been taken to trace copyright holders. However, if there have been unintentional omissions or failure to trace copyright holders, we apologize and will, if informed, endeavor to make corrections in any future edition.

Key: *b* = bottom, *c* = center, *l* = left, *r* = right, *t* = top

Cover *front cover* Getty/AFP*;* Page 1 Photolibrary Erik Aeder; 2–3 iStockphoto; 4–5 Corbis/James Reeve; 7 PA/EMP; 8*tl* Getty/Hulton; 9*br* Barber Nichols, Inc.; 10*l* Getty/Hulton; 10*b* Corbis/Bettman; 11*tr* NASA; 11*b* USAF; 12*tl* LAT Photographic; 12–13 Corbis/Schlegelmilch; 13*tr* Corbis/David Madison; 14*l* Corbis; 14–15 Sutton Motorsports Images; 15*tr* Getty/AFP; 16*tl* Herrenknecht AG, Germany; 16–17 Science Photo Library/Tony Craddock; 17*tr* Caterpillar, Inc.; 18 Shutterstock; 19*t* Getty/AFP/STR; 19*b* Alamy/ David Noble; 20*tl* PA Photos; 20–21 National Geographic Images; 22 NASA; 23*t* PA/AP; 23*b* Corbis/ Karen Kasmauski; 24–25 Shutterstock; 24*cl* SNCF Alstom Transport, France; 25*tl* Alamy/Peter Widmann; 26–27 Rex Features/Sipa Press; 27*tr* Shutterstock; 27*bl* PA/AP; 28*tl* Chris Carr; 28*lc* Fred Rompelberg, 28–29 Corbis/Tim de Waele; 29*b* Emilio Scotto; 30 Getty/Hulton; 31 PA/AP; 32*tl* Getty/Hulton; 32–33 PA/AP; 33*tl* Ken Warby; 33*tr* Philip Plisson, France; 34–35 Getty/Stone; 34*bl* Diogo Guerreiro and Flávio Jardim (Expedition DestinoAzul); 35*tr* Ian Edmondson/Barefoot Media; 36*cl* PA/AP; 36–37 Getty/ AFP/Torsten Blackwood; 37*tr* Millennium Super Yachts; 38–39 Royal Caribbean International; 40*tl* Ben and Elinore Carlin; 40–41 Rinspeed, Inc., Switzerland; 41*t* Sealegs Corp. NZ; 41*b* Corbis/epa; 42 Alcoa, Inc.; 43 Carnegie Mellon University; 44 Getty/Hulton; 45 NASA/Dryden; 46–47 Corbis/Philip Wallick; 48*cl* Getty/AFP; 49*tr* Corbis/How Hwee Young; 49*br* Getty/AFP; 50*tl* Bob Holloway; 50–51 Corbis/ Firefly Productions; 51*br* Juergen Lehle; 52*tl* PA/AP; 52–53 PA/AP; 54*bl* PA/AP; 54–55 PA/AP; 55*tr* PA/AP; 55br Joseph Kittinger; 56*tl* ESA/NASA; 56*cr* Corbis/Roger Ressmeyer; 56*bl* NASA; 57 NASA; 58 PA/AP; 59 Shutterstock; 60*bl* Getty/Fred Tanneau/AFP; 60*tr* PA/AP; 61 Corbis/ Schlegelmilch; 62–63 iStockphoto; 64 Getty/Daniel Forster/AFP

The publisher would like to thank the following illustrators:
Steven Weston (Linden Artists) 8–9; Encompass Graphics 21, 34;
Peter Winfield 25, 52; Sebastian Quigley (Linden Artists) 42–43, 48–49